YOUR PERSONAL
HOROSCOPE
2018

VIRGO

D0660151

YOUR PERSONAL HOROSCOPE 2018

VIRGO

24th August–23rd September

igloobooks

Published in 2017
by Igloo Books Ltd
Cottage Farm
Sywell
NN6 0BJ
www.igloobooks.com

Copyright © 2017 Foulsham Publishing Ltd

Produced for Igloo Books by Foulsham Publishing Ltd, The Old Barrel Store,
Drayman's Lane, Marlow, Bucks SL7 2FF, England

FIR003 0717
2 4 6 8 10 9 7 5 3 1
ISBN: 978-1-78670-887-8

This is an abridged version of material originally published
in Old Moore's Horoscope and Astral Diary.

Cover design by Charles Wood-Penn
Edited by Jasmin Peppiatt

Printed and manufactured in China

CONTENTS

CONTENTS

INTRODUCTION

Your Personal Horoscopes have been specifically created to allow you to get the most from astrological patterns and the way they have a bearing on not only your zodiac sign, but nuances within it. Using the diary section of the book you can read about the influences and possibilities of each and every day of the year. It will be possible for you to see when you are likely to be cheerful and happy or those times when your nature is in retreat and you will be more circumspect. The diary will help to give you a feel for the specific 'cycles' of astrology and the way they can subtly change your day-to-day life. For example, when you see the sign ☿, this means that the planet Mercury is retrograde at that time. Retrograde means it appears to be running backwards through the zodiac. Such a happening has a significant effect on communication skills, but this is only one small aspect of how the Personal Horoscope can help you.

With Your Personal Horoscope the story doesn't end with the diary pages. It includes simple ways for you to work out the zodiac sign the Moon occupied at the time of your birth, and what this means for your personality. In addition, if you know the time of day you were born, it is possible to discover your Ascendant, yet another important guide to your personal make-up and potential.

Many readers are interested in relationships and in knowing how well they get on with people of other astrological signs. You might also be interested in the way you appear to very different sorts of individuals. If you are such a person, the section on Venus will be of particular interest. Despite the rapidly changing position of this planet, you can work out your Venus sign, and learn what bearing it will have on your life.

Using Your Personal Horoscope you can travel on one of the most fascinating and rewarding journeys that anyone can take – the journey to a better realisation of self.

THE ESSENCE
OF VIRGO

Exploring the Personality of
Virgo the Virgin

(24TH AUGUST – 23RD SEPTEMBER)

What's in a sign?

Virgo people tend to be a rather extraordinary sort of mixture. Your ruling planet is Mercury, which makes you inclined to be rather chatty and quite sociable. On the other hand, yours is known as an Earth-ruled zodiac sign, which is usually steady and sometimes quite reserved. Thus, from the start, there are opposing energies ruling your life. This is not a problem when the right sort of balance is achieved and that is what you are looking for all the time. Repressed social and personal communication can make you worrisome, which in turn leads to a slightly fussy tendency that is not your most endearing quality.

At best you are quite ingenious and can usually rely on your strong intuition when weighing up the pros and cons of any given situation. Like all Earth signs you are able to accrue wealth and work hard to achieve your ultimate objectives in life. However, one is left with the impression that problems arise for Virgo when acquisition takes over. In other words, you need to relax more and to enjoy the fruits of your successes on a more regular basis.

Tidiness is important to you, and not just around your home. You particularly don't like loose ends and can be meticulous in your sense of detail. It seems likely that the fictional Sherlock Holmes was a Virgo subject and his ability to get to the absolute root of all situations is a stock-in-trade for the sign of the Virgin. Flexibility is especially important in relationships and you shouldn't become so obsessed with the way surroundings look that you fail to make the most of social opportunities.

Another tendency for Virgo is a need to 'keep up with the Joneses'. Why do you do this? Mainly because like your fellow Mercury-ruled sign of Gemini you haven't really as much confidence

9

as seems to be the case. As a result you want to know that you are as good as anyone else, and if possible better. This can, on occasion, lead to a sort of subconscious race that you can never hope to win. Learn to relax and to recognise when you are on top anyway, and you are really motoring.

Virgo resources

Virgoan people are not at all short of savvy and one of the most important considerations about your make-up is that you usually know how to proceed in a practical sense. At your disposal you have an armoury of weapons that can lead to a successful sort of life, especially in a practical and financial sense.

Your ruling planet, Mercury, makes you a good communicator and shows you the way to get on-side with the world at large. This quality means that you are rarely short of the right sort of information that is necessary in order to get things right first time. Where this doesn't prove to be possible, you have Earth-sign tenacity and an ability to work extremely hard for long hours in order to achieve your intended objectives. On the way, you tend on the whole to make friends, though you might find it hard to get through life without picking up one or two adversaries too.

Virgo people are capable of being gregarious and gossipy, whilst at the same time retaining an internal discipline which more perceptive people are inclined to recognise instinctively. You cement secure friendships and that means nearly always having someone to rely on in times of difficulty. But this isn't a one-way street, because you are a very supportive type yourself and would fight tenaciously on behalf of a person or a cause that you supported wholeheartedly. At such times you can appear to be quite brave, even though you could be quaking inside.

A tendency towards being nervy is not always as evident as you might think, mainly because you have the power and ability to keep it behind closed doors. Retaining the secrets of friends, despite your tendency to indulge in gossip, is an important part of your character and is the reason that others learn to trust you. Organisational skills are good and you love to sort out the puzzles of life, which makes you ideal for tedious jobs that many other people would find impossible to complete. Your curiosity knows no bounds and you would go to almost any length to answer questions that are uppermost in your mind at any point in time.

Beneath the surface

So what are you really like? Well, in the case of Virgo this might be the most interesting journey of all, and one that could deeply surprise even some of those people who think they know you very well indeed. First of all, it must be remembered that your ruling planet is Mercury, known as the lord of communication. As a result, it's important for you to keep in touch with the world at large. That's fine, except for the fact that your Earth-sign tendencies are inclined to make you basically quiet by nature.

Here we find something of a contradiction and one that leads to more than a few misunderstandings. You are particularly sensitive to little changes out there in the cosmos and so can be much more voluble on some days than on others. The result can be that others see you as being somewhat moody, which isn't really the case at all. You are inclined to be fairly nervy and would rarely be quite as confident as you give the impression of being. Although usually robust in terms of general health, this doesn't always seem to be the case and a tendency towards a slightly hypochondriac nature can be the result. Some Virgoans can make an art form out of believing that they are unwell and you need to understand that part of the reason for this lies in your desire for attention.

Another accusation that is levelled at Virgoans is that they are inclined to be fussy over details. This is also an expression of your lack of basic confidence in yourself. For some reason you subconsciously assume that if every last matter is dealt with absolutely, all will work out well. In reality the more relaxed you remain, the better you find your ability to cope with everyday life.

The simple truth is that you are much more capable than your inner nature tends to believe and could easily think more of yourself than you do. You have a logical mind, but also gain from the intuition that is possessed by all Mercury-ruled individuals. The more instinctive you become, the less you worry about things and the more relaxed life can seem to be. You also need to override a natural suspicion of those around you. Trust is a hard thing for you, but a very important one.

Making the best of yourself

There are many ways in which you can exploit the best potentials of your zodiac sign and, at the same time, play down some of the less favourable possibilities. From the very start, it's important to realise that the main criticism that comes your way from the outside world is that you are too fussy by half. So, simply avoid being critical of others and the way they do things. By all means stick to your own opinions, but avoid forcing them onto other people. If you can get over this hurdle, your personal popularity will already be that much greater. If people love you, you care for them in return – it's as simple as that, because at heart you aren't really very complicated.

Despite the fact that a little humility would go a long way, you also do need to remain sure of yourself. There's no real problem in allowing others their head, while following your own opinions all the same. Use your practical skills to the full and don't rush things just because other people seem to do so. Although you are ruled by quick Mercury, you also come from an Earth sign, which means steady progress.

Find outlets to desensitise your over-nervy nature. You can do this with plenty of healthy exercise and by taking an interest in subject matter that isn't of any great importance, but which you find appealing all the same. Avoid concentrating too much on any one thing, because that is the road to paranoia.

Realise that you have an innate sense of what is right and that, if it is utilised in the right way, you can make gains for yourself and for the people you love. You have a good fund of ideas, so don't be afraid to use them. Most importantly of all, you need to remain confident but flexible. That's the path to popularity – something you need much more than you might realise.

The impressions you give

This can be something of a problem area to at least some people born under the zodiac sign of Virgo. There isn't much doubt that your heart is in the right place and this fact isn't lost on many observers. All the same, you can appear to be very definite in your opinions, even to the point of stubbornness, and you won't give ground when you know you are in the right. A slight problem here might be that Virgoans nearly always think they have the moral and legal high ground. In the majority of cases this may indeed be true, but there are ways and means of putting the message across.

What Virgo needs more than anything else is tact. A combination of Mercury, ruling your means of communication, and your Earth-sign heritage can, on occasions, make you appear to be rather blunt. Mercury also aids in quick thinking and problem solving. The sum total can make it appear that you don't take other people's opinions into account and that you are prepared to railroad your ideas through if necessary.

Most people recognise that you are very capable and may therefore automatically turn to you for leadership. It isn't certain how you will react under any given circumstance because although you can criticise others, your Earth-sign proclivities don't make you a natural leader. In a strong supportive role you can be wonderful and it is towards this scenario that you might choose to look.

Avoid people accusing you of being fussy by deliberately cultivating flexibility in your thinking and your actions. You are one of the kindest and most capable people to be found anywhere in the zodiac. All you need to do to complete the picture is to let the world at large know what you are. With your natural kindness and your ability to get things done, you can show yourself to be a really attractive individual. Look towards a brush-up of your public persona. Deep inside you are organised and caring, though a little nervy. Let people know exactly what you are – it only makes you more human.

The way forward

Before anyone can move forward into anything it is important for them to realise exactly where they are now. In your case this is especially true. Probably the most problematic area of Virgo is in realising not what is being done but rather why. It is the inability to ask this question on a regular basis that leads Virgo into a rut now and again. Habit isn't simply a word to many people born under the zodiac sign of Virgo, it's a religion. The strange thing about this fact is that if you find yourself catapulted, against your will, into a different sort of routine, you soon learn to adopt it as if it were second nature. In other words this way of behaving is endemic, but not necessarily inevitable. The way out of it is simple and comes thanks to your ruling planet of Mercury. Keep talking, but at the same time listen. Adapt your life on a regular basis and say 'So many habits are not necessary', at least ten times a day.

All the same, it wouldn't be very prudent to throw out the baby with the bath water. Your ability to stick at things is justifiably legendary. This generally means that you arrive at your desired destination in life, even though it might take you a long time to get there. The usual result is respect from people who don't have your persistence or tenacity.

With regard to love and affection, you are in a good position to place a protecting blanket around those you love the most. This is fine, as long as you check regularly that you are not suffocating them with it. If you allow a certain degree of freedom, people will respect your concern all the more and they won't fight against it. By all means, communicate your affection and don't allow your natural Earth-sign reserve to get in the way of expressing feelings that are quite definite internally. This is another aspect of letting the world know what you are really like and is of crucial importance to your zodiac sign.

You need variety and if possible an absence of worry. Only when things are going wrong do Virgoans become the fussy individuals that sometimes attract a little criticism. As long as you feel that you are in charge of your own destiny, you can remain optimistic – another vital requisite for Virgo. With just a little effort you can be one of the most popular and loved people around. Add to this your natural ability to succeed and the prognosis for the sign of the Virgin is very good.

VIRGO ON THE CUSP

Astrological profiles are altered for those people born at either the beginning or the end of a zodiac sign, or, more properly, on the cusps of a sign. In the case of Leo this would be on the 24th of August and for two or three days after, and similarly at the end of the sign, probably from the 21st to the 23rd of September.

The Leo Cusp – August 24th to 26th

If anything is designed to lighten the load of being a Virgoan, it's having a Leo quality in the nature too. All Virgoans are inclined to take themselves too seriously on occasions and they don't have half as much self-esteem as they could really use effectively. Being born on the Leo cusp gives better self-confidence, less of the supreme depths which Virgo alone can display and a much more superficial view of many aspects of life. The material success for which Virgo is famous probably won't be lacking, but there will also be a determination to have fun and let the bright, aspiring qualities that are so popular in the Leo character show.

In matters of love, you are likely to be easy-going, bright, bubbly and always willing to have a laugh. You relish good company and though you sometimes go at things like a bull at a gate, your intentions are true and you know how to get others to like you a great deal. Family matters are right up your street, because not only do you have the ability to put down firm and enduring roots, but you are the most staunch and loyal protector of family values that anyone could wish for.

When it comes to working, you seem to have the best combination of all. You have the ability to work long and hard, achieving your objectives as all Virgoans do, but managing to do so with a smile permanently fixed to your face. You are naturally likely to find yourself at the head of things, where your combination of skills is going to be of the greatest use. This sign combination is to be found in every nook and cranny of the working world but perhaps less frequently in jobs which involve getting your hands dirty.

There are times when you definitely live on your nerves and when you don't get the genuine relaxation that the Virgoan qualities within you demand. Chances are you are much more robust than you consider yourself to be and, as long as you keep busy most of the time, you tend to enjoy a contented life. The balance usually works well, because Leo lifts Virgo, whilst Virgo stabilises an often too superficial Lion.

The Libra Cusp – September 21st to 23rd

Virgo responds well to input from other parts of the zodiac and probably never more so than in the case of the Libran cusp. The reasons for this are very simple: what Virgo on its own lacks, Libra possesses, and it's the same on the other side of the coin. Libra is often flighty and doesn't take enough time to rest, but it is compensated by the balance inherent in the sign, so it weighs things carefully. Virgo on the other hand is deep and sometimes dark, but because it's ruled by capricious little Mercury, it can also be rather too impetuous. The potential break-even point is obvious and usually leads to a fairly easy-going individual, who is intellectual, thoughtful and practical when necessary.

You are a great person to have around in good times and bad, and you know how to have fun. A staunch support and helper to your friends, you enjoy a high degree of popularity, which usually extends to affairs of the heart. There may be more than one of these in your life and it's best for people born on this cusp not to marry in haste or too early in life. Even if you get things wrong first time around, you have the ability to bounce back quickly and don't become easily discouraged. It is good for you to be often in the company of gregarious and interesting people, but you are quite capable of surviving on your own when you have to.

Health matters may be on your mind more than is strictly necessary and it's true that you can sometimes worry yourself into minor ailments that would not otherwise have existed. It is important for you to get plenty of rest and also to enjoy yourself. The more you work on behalf of others, the less time you spend thinking about your own possible ailments. Anxiety needs to be avoided, often by getting to the root of a problem and solving it quickly.

A capable and committed worker, you are at your best when able to share the decisions, but you are quite reliable when you have to make up your mind alone. You would never bully those beneath you. You are never short of support and you bring joy to life most of the time.

VIRGO AND ITS ASCENDANTS

The nature of every individual on the planet is composed of the rich variety of zodiac signs and planetary positions that were present at the time of their birth. Your Sun sign, which in your case is Virgo, is one of the many factors when it comes to assessing the unique person you are. Probably the most important consideration, other than your Sun sign, is to establish the zodiac sign that was rising over the eastern horizon at the time that you were born. This is your Ascending or Rising sign. Most popular astrology fails to take account of the Ascendant, and yet its importance remains with you from the very moment of your birth, through every day of your life. The Ascendant is evident in the way you approach the world, and so, when meeting a person for the first time, it is this astrological influence that you are most likely to notice first. Our Ascending sign essentially represents what we appear to be, while the Sun sign is what we feel inside ourselves.

The Ascendant also has the potential for modifying our overall nature. For example, if you were born at a time of day when Virgo was passing over the eastern horizon (this would be around the time of dawn) then you would be classed as a double Virgo. As such, you would typify this zodiac sign, both internally and in your dealings with others. However, if your Ascendant sign turned out to be a Fire sign, such as Aries, there would be a profound alteration of nature, away from the expected qualities of Virgo.

One of the reasons why popular astrology often ignores the Ascendant is that it has always been rather difficult to establish. We have found a way to make this possible by devising an easy-to-use table, which you will find on page 157 of this book. Using this, you can establish your Ascendant sign at a glance. You will need to know your rough time of birth, then it is simply a case of following the instructions.

For those readers who have no idea of their time of birth, it might be worth allowing a good friend, or perhaps your partner, to read through the section that follows this introduction. Someone who deals with you on a regular basis may easily discover your Ascending sign, even though you could have some difficulty establishing it for yourself. A good understanding of this component of your nature is essential if you want to be aware of that 'other person' who is responsible for the way you make contact with the world at large. Your Sun sign, Ascendant sign, and the other pointers in this book will, together, allow you a far better understanding of what makes you tick as an individual. Peeling back the different layers of your astrological make-up can be an enlightening experience and the Ascendant may represent one of the most important layers of all.

Virgo with Virgo Ascendant

You get the best of both worlds, and on rare occasions the worst too. Frighteningly efficient, you have the ability to scare people with your constant knack of getting it right. This won't endear you to everyone, particularly those who pride themselves on being disorganised. You make a loyal friend and would do almost anything for someone who is important to you, though you do so in a quiet way because you are not the most noisy of types. Chances are that you possess the ability to write well and you also have a cultured means of verbal communication on those occasions when you really choose to speak out.

It isn't difficult for you to argue your case, though much of the time you refuse to do so and can lock yourself into your own private world for days on end. If you are at ease with yourself you possess a powerful personality, which you can express well. Conversely, you can live on your nerves and cause problems for yourself. Meditation is good, fussing over details that really don't matter at all is less useful. Once you have chosen a particular course of action there are few people around with sufficient will-power to prevent you from getting what you want. Wide open spaces where the hand of nature is all around can make you feel very relaxed.

Virgo with Libra Ascendant

Libra has the ability to lighten almost any load and it is particularly good at doing so when it is brought together with the much more repressed sign of Virgo. To the world at large you seem relaxed, happy and able to cope with most of the pressures that life places upon you. Not only do you deal with your own life in a bright and breezy manner but you are usually on hand to help others out of any dilemma that they might make for themselves. With excellent powers of communication you leave the world at large in no doubt whatsoever concerning both your opinions and your wishes. It is in the talking stakes that you really excel because Virgo brings the silver tongue of Mercury and Libra adds the Air-sign desire to be in constant touch with the world outside your door.

You like to have a good time and are often found in the company of interesting and stimulating people, who have the ability to bring out the very best in your bright and sparkling personality. Underneath however, there is still much of the worrying Virgoan to be found and this means that you have to learn to relax inside as well as appearing to do so externally. In fact, you are much more complex than most people would realise and definitely would not be suited to a life that allowed you too much time to think about yourself.

Virgo with Scorpio Ascendant

This is intensity carried through to the absolute. If you have a problem, it is that you fail to externalise all that is going on inside that deep, bubbling cauldron of your inner self. Realising what you are capable of is not a problem, these only start when you have to make it plain to those around you what you want. Part of the reason for this is that you don't always understand yourself. You love intensely and would do absolutely anything for a person you are fond of, even though you might have to inconvenience yourself a great deal on the way. Relationships can cause you slight problems however, since you need to associate with people who at least come somewhere near to understanding what makes you tick. If you manage to bridge the gap between yourself and the world that constantly knocks on your door, you show yourself to be powerful, magnetic and compulsive.

There are times when you definitely prefer to stay quiet, though you do have a powerful ability to get your message across when you think it is necessary to do so. There are people around who might think that you are a push-over, but they could easily get a shock when you sense that the time is right to answer back. You probably have a very orderly house and don't care for clutter of any sort.

Virgo with Sagittarius Ascendant

This is a combination that might look rather odd at first sight because these two signs have so very little in common. However, the saying goes that opposites attract and in terms of the personality you display to the world this is especially true in your case. Not everyone understands what makes you tick but you try to show the least complicated face to the world that you can manage to display. You can be deep and secretive on occasions, and yet at other times you can start talking as soon as you climb out of bed and never stop until you are back there again. Inspirational and spontaneous, you take the world by storm on those occasions when you are free from worries and firing on all cylinders. It is a fact that you support your friends, though there are rather more of them than would be the case for Virgo taken on its own and you don't always choose them as wisely as you might.

There are times when you display a temper and although Sagittarius is incapable of bearing a grudge, the same cannot be said for Virgo, which has a better memory than the elephant. For the best results in life you need to relax as much as possible and avoid overheating that powerful and busy brain. Virgo gives you the ability to concentrate on one thing at once, a skill you should encourage.

Virgo with Capricorn Ascendant

Your endurance, persistence and concentration are legendary and there is virtually nothing that eludes you once you have the bit between your teeth. You are not the pushy, fussy, go-getting sort of Virgoan but are steady, methodical and very careful. Once you have made up your mind, a whole team of wild horses could not change it and although this can be a distinct blessing at times, it is a quality that can bring odd problems into your life too. The difficulty starts when you adopt a lost or less than sensible cause. Even in the face of overwhelming evidence that you are wrong, there is something inside you that prevents any sort of U-turn and so you walk forward as solidly as only you are able, to a destination that won't suit you at all.

There are few people around who are more loyal and constant than you can be. There is a lighter and brighter side to your nature and the one or two people who are most important in your life will know how to bring it out. You have a wicked sense of humour, particularly if you have had a drink or when you are feeling on top form. Travel does you the world of good, even if there is a part of you that would rather stay at home. You have a potent, powerful and magnetic personality but for much of the time it is kept carefully hidden.

Virgo with Aquarius Ascendant

How could anyone make convention unconventional? Well, if anyone can manage, you can. There are great contradictions here because on the one hand you always want to do what is expected, but the Aquarian quality within your nature loves to surprise everyone on the way. If you don't always know what you are thinking or doing, it's a pretty safe bet that others won't either, so it's important on occasions to stop and really think. However, this is not a pressing concern because you tend to live a fairly happy life and muddle through no matter what. Other people tend to take to you well and it is likely that you will have many friends. You tend to be bright and cheerful and can approach even difficult tasks with the certainty that you have the skills necessary to see them through to their conclusion. Give and take are important factors in the life of any individual and particularly so in your case. Because you can stretch yourself in order to understand what makes other people think and act in the way that they do, you have the reputation of being a good friend and a reliable colleague.

In love you can be somewhat more fickle than the typical Virgoan and yet you are always interesting to live with. Where you are, things happen and you mix a sparkling wit with deep insights.

Virgo with Pisces Ascendant

You might have been accused on occasions of being too sensitive for your own good, a charge that is not entirely without foundation. Certainly you are very understanding of the needs of others, sometimes to the extent that you put everything aside to help them. This would also be true in the case of charities, for you care very much about the world and the people who cling tenaciously to its surface. Your ability to love on a one-to-one basis knows no bounds though you may not discriminate as much as you could, particularly when young, and might have one or two false starts in the love stakes. You don't always choose to verbalise your thoughts and this can cause problems, because there is always so much going on in your mind and Virgo especially needs good powers of communication. Pisces is quieter and you need to force yourself to say what you think when the explanation is important.

You would never betray a confidence and sometimes take on rather more for the sake of your friends than is strictly good for you. This is not a fault but can cause you problems all the same. Because you are so intuitive, there is little that escapes your attention, though you should avoid being pessimistic about your insights. Changes of scenery suit you and extensive travel would bring out the best in what can be a repressed nature at times.

Virgo with Aries Ascendant

Virgo is steady and sure, though also fussy and stubborn. Aries is fast and determined, restless and active. It can be seen already that this is a rather strange meeting of characteristics and because Virgo is ruled by capricious Mercury, the result will change from hour to hour and day to day. It isn't merely that others find it difficult to know where they are with you; they can't even understand what makes you tick. This will make you the subject of endless fascination and attention, at which you will be apparently surprised but inwardly pleased. If anyone ever really gets to know what goes on in that busy mind, they may find the implications very difficult to deal with and it is a fact that only you would have the ability to live inside your crowded head.

As a partner and a parent you are second to none, though you would tend to get on better with your children once they started to grow, since by this time you may be slightly less restricting to their own desires, which will often clash with your own on their behalf. You are capable of give and take and could certainly not be considered selfish, though your desire to get the best from everyone might be misconstrued on occasion.

Virgo with Taurus Ascendant

This combination tends to amplify the Taurean qualities that you naturally possess and this is the case because both Taurus and Virgo are Earth signs. However, there are certain factors related to Virgo that show themselves very differently than the sign's cousin Taurus. Virgo is more fussy, nervy and pedantic than Taurus and all of these qualities are going to show up in your nature at one level or another. On the plus side you might be slightly less concerned about having a perfect home and a perfect family and your interest in life appears at a more direct level than that of the true Taurean. You care very much about your home and family and are very loyal to your friends. It's true that you sometimes tend to try and take them over and you can also show a marked tendency to dominate, but your heart is in the right place and most people recognise that your caring is genuine.

One problem is that there are very few shades of grey in your life, which is certainly not the case for other zodiac sign combinations. Living your life in the way that you do, there isn't much room for compromise and this fact alone can prove to be something of a problem where relationships are concerned. In a personal sense you need a partner who is willing to be organised and one who relies on your judgements, which don't change all that often.

Virgo with Gemini Ascendant

A Gemini Ascendant means that you are ruled by Mercury, both through your Sun sign and through the sign that was rising at the time of your birth. This means that words are your basic tools in life and you use them to the full. Some writers have this combination, because even speaking to people virtually all the time is not enough. Although you have many friends you are fairly high-minded, which means that you can make enemies too. The fact is that people either care very much for you, or else they don't like you at all. This can be difficult for you to come to terms with because you don't really set out to cause friction – it simply attracts itself to you.

Although you love travel, home is important too and there is a basic insecurity in your nature that comes about as a result of an overdose of Mercury, which makes you nervy and sometimes far less confident than anyone would guess. Success in your life may be slower arriving with this combination because you are determined to achieve your objectives on your own terms and this can take time. Always a contradiction, often a puzzle to others, your ultimate happiness in life is directly proportional to the effort you put in, though this should not mean wearing yourself out on the way.

Virgo with Cancer Ascendant

What can this union of zodiac signs bring to the party that isn't there in either Virgo or Cancer alone? Well quite a bit actually. Virgo can be very fussy on occasions and too careful for its own good. The presence of steady, serene Cancer alters the perspectives and allows a smoother, more flowing Virgoan to greet the world. You are chatty, easy to know and exhibit a combination of the practical skills of Virgo, together with the deep and penetrating insights that are typical of Cancer. This can make you appear to be very powerful and your insights are second to none. You are a born organiser and love to be where things are happening, even if you are only there to help make the sandwiches or to pour the tea. Invariably your role will be much greater but you don't seek personal acclaim and are a good team player on most occasions.

There is a quiet side to your nature and those who live with you will eventually get used to your need for solitude. This seems strange because Virgo is generally such a chatterbox and, taken on its own, is rarely quiet for long. In love you show great affection and a sense of responsibility that makes you an ideal parent, though it is possible sometimes that you care rather more than you are willing to show.

Virgo with Leo Ascendant

Here we have cheerfulness allied to efficiency, which can be a very positive combination most of the time. With all the sense of honour, justice and bravery of the Leo subject, Virgo adds staying power through tedious situations and offers you a slightly more serious view of life than we would expect from the Lion alone. In almost any situation you can keep going until you get to your chosen destination and you also find the time to reach out to the people who need your unique nature the most. Few would deny your kindness, though you can attract a little envy because it seems as though yours is the sort of personality that everyone else wants.

Most people born with this combination have a radiant smile and will do their best to think situations through carefully. If there is a tendency to be foolhardy, it is carefully masked beneath a covering of Virgoan common sense. Family matters are dealt with efficiently and with great love. Some might see you as close one moment and distant the next. The truth is that you are always on the go and have a thousand different things to think about, all at the same time. On the whole your presence is noticed and you may represent the most loyal friend of them all.

THE MOON AND THE PART IT PLAYS IN YOUR LIFE

In astrology the Moon is probably the single most important heavenly body after the Sun. Its unique position, as partner to the Earth on its journey around the solar system, means that the Moon appears to pass through the signs of the zodiac extremely quickly. The zodiac position of the Moon at the time of your birth plays a great part in personal character and is especially significant in the build-up of your emotional nature.

Your Own Moon Sign

Discovering the position of the Moon at the time of your birth has always been notoriously difficult because tracking the complex zodiac positions of the Moon is not easy. This process has been reduced to three simple stages with our Lunar Tables. A breakdown of the Moon's zodiac positions can be found from page 35 onwards, so that once you know what your Moon Sign is, you can see what part this plays in the overall build-up of your personal character.

If you follow the instructions on the next page you will soon be able to work out exactly what zodiac sign the Moon occupied on the day that you were born and you can then go on to compare the reading for this position with those of your Sun sign and your Ascendant. It is partly the comparison between these three important positions that goes towards making you the unique individual you are.

HOW TO DISCOVER YOUR MOON SIGN

This is a three-stage process. You may need a pen and a piece of paper but if you follow the instructions below the process should only take a minute or so.

STAGE 1 First of all you need to know the Moon Age at the time of your birth. If you look at Moon Table 1, on page 33, you will find all the years between 1920 and 2018 down the left side. Find the year of your birth and then trace across to the right to the month of your birth. Where the two intersect you will find a number. This is the date of the New Moon in the month that you were born. You now need to count forward the number of days between the New Moon and your own birthday. For example, if the New Moon in the month of your birth was shown as being the 6th and you were born on the 20th, your Moon Age Day would be 14. If the New Moon in the month of your birth came after your birthday, you need to count forward from the New Moon in the previous month. Whatever the result, jot this number down so that you do not forget it.

STAGE 2 Take a look at Moon Table 2 on page 34. Down the left hand column look for the date of your birth. Now trace across to the month of your birth. Where the two meet you will find a letter. Copy this letter down alongside your Moon Age Day.

STAGE 3 Moon Table 3 on page 34 will supply you with the zodiac sign the Moon occupied on the day of your birth. Look for your Moon Age Day down the left hand column and then for the letter you found in Stage 2. Where the two converge you will find a zodiac sign and this is the sign occupied by the Moon on the day that you were born.

Your Zodiac Moon Sign Explained

You will find a profile of all zodiac Moon Signs on pages 35 to 38, showing in yet another way how astrology helps to make you into the individual that you are. In each daily entry of the Astral Diary you can find the zodiac position of the Moon for every day of the year. This also allows you to discover your lunar birthdays. Since the Moon passes through all the signs of the zodiac in about a month, you can expect something like twelve lunar birthdays each year. At these times you are likely to be emotionally steady and able to make the sort of decisions that have real, lasting value.

MOON TABLE 1

YEAR	JUL	AUG	SEP	YEAR	JUL	AUG	SEP	YEAR	JUL	AUG	SEP
1920	15	14	12	1953	11	9	8	1986	7	5	4
1921	5	3	2	1954	29	28	27	1987	25	24	23
1922	24	22	21	1955	19	17	16	1988	13	12	11
1923	14	12	10	1956	8	6	4	1989	3 1/31	29	
1924	2/31	30	28	1957	27	25	23	1990	22	20	19
1925	20	19	18	1958	16	15	13	1991	11	9	8
1926	9	8	7	1959	6	4	3	1992	29	28	26
1927	28	27	25	1960	24	22	21	1993	19	17	16
1928	17	16	14	1961	12	11	10	1994	8	7	5
1929	6	5	3	1962	1/31	30	28	1995	27	26	24
1930	25	24	22	1963	20	19	17	1996	15	14	13
1931	15	13	12	1964	9	7	6	1997	4	3	2
1932	3	2/31	30	1965	28	26	25	1998	23	22	20
1933	22	21	19	1966	17	16	14	1999	13	11	10
1934	11	10	9	1967	7	5	4	2000	1/31	29	27
1935	30	29	27	1968	25	24	23	2001	20	19	17
1936	18	17	15	1969	13	12	11	2002	9	8	6
1937	8	6	4	1970	4	2	1	2003	28	27	26
1938	27	25	23	1971	22	20	19	2004	16	14	13
1939	16	15	13	1972	11	9	8	2005	6	4	3
1940	5	4	2	1973	29	28	27	2006	25	23	22
1941	24	22	21	1974	19	17	16	2007	15	13	12
1942	13	12	10	1975	9	7	5	2008	31	31	30
1943	2 1/30	29		1976	27	25	23	2009	22	20	19
1944	20	18	17	1977	16	14	13	2010	12	10	8
1945	9	8	6	1978	5	4	2	2011	2/31	29	27
1946	28	26	25	1979	24	22	21	2012	19	17	16
1947	17	16	14	1980	12	11	10	2013	7	6	4
1948	6	5	3	1981	1/31	29	28	2014	25	24	23
1949	25	24	23	1982	20	19	17	2015	16	15	13
1950	15	13	12	1983	10	8	7	2016	4	2	1
1951	4	2	1	1984	28	26	25	2017	23	22	20
1952	23	20	19	1985	17	16	14	2018	13	11	9

TABLE 2   MOON TABLE 3

DAY	AUG	SEP	M/D	U	V	W	X	Y	Z	a
1	U	X	0	LE	LE	LE	VI	VI	LI	LI
2	U	X	1	LE	VI	VI	VI	LI	LI	LI
3	V	X	2	VI	VI	VI	LI	LI	LI	LI
4	V	Y	3	VI	VI	LI	LI	LI	SC	SC
5	V	Y	4	LI	LI	LI	LI	SC	SC	SC
6	V	Y	5	LI	LI	SC	SC	SC	SC	SA
7	V	Y	6	LI	SC	SC	SC	SA	SA	SA
8	V	Y	7	SC	SC	SA	SA	SA	SA	SA
9	V	Y	8	SC	SC	SA	SA	SA	CP	CP
10	V	Y	9	SA	SA	SA	SA	CP	CP	CP
11	V	Y	10	SA	SA	CP	CP	CP	CP	AQ
12	V	Y	11	CP	CP	CP	CP	AQ	AQ	AQ
13	V	Y	12	CP	CP	AQ	AQ	AQ	AQ	PI
14	W	Z	13	CP	CP	AQ	AQ	AQ	PI	PI
15	W	Z	14	AQ	AQ	PI	PI	PI	PI	AR
16	W	Z	15	AQ	AQ	PI	PI	PI	PI	AR
17	W	Z	16	AQ	PI	PI	PI	AR	AR	AR
18	W	Z	17	PI	PI	PI	AR	AR	AR	AR
19	W	Z	18	PI	PI	AR	AR	AR	AR	TA
20	W	Z	19	PI	AR	AR	AR	TA	TA	TA
21	W	Z	20	AR	AR	TA	TA	TA	TA	GE
22	W	Z	21	AR	TA	TA	TA	GE	GE	GE
23	W	Z	22	TA	TA	TA	GE	GE	GE	GE
24	X	a	23	TA	TA	GE	GE	GE	GE	CA
25	X	a	24	TA	GE	GE	GE	CA	CA	CA
26	X	a	25	GE	GE	CA	CA	CA	CA	CA
27	X	a	26	GE	CA	CA	CA	LE	LE	LE
28	X	a	27	CA	CA	CA	LE	LE	LE	LE
29	X	a	28	CA	CA	LE	LE	LE	LE	VI
30	X	a	29	CA	LE	LE	LE	VI	VI	VI
31	X	–								

AR = Aries, TA = Taurus, GE = Gemini, CA = Cancer, LE = Leo, VI = Virgo,
LI = Libra, SC = Scorpio, SA = Sagittarius, CP = Capricorn, AQ = Aquarius, PI = Pisces

MOON SIGNS

Moon in Aries

You have a strong imagination, courage, determination and a desire to do things in your own way and forge your own path through life.

Originality is a key attribute; you are seldom stuck for ideas although your mind is changeable and you could take the time to focus on individual tasks. Often quick-tempered, you take orders from few people and live life at a fast pace. Avoid health problems by taking regular time out for rest and relaxation.

Emotionally, it is important that you talk to those you are closest to and work out your true feelings. Once you discover that people are there to help, there is less necessity for you to do everything yourself.

Moon in Taurus

The Moon in Taurus gives you a courteous and friendly manner, which means you are likely to have many friends.

The good things in life mean a lot to you, as Taurus is an Earth sign that delights in experiences which please the senses. Hence you are probably a lover of good food and drink, which may in turn mean you need to keep an eye on the bathroom scales, especially as looking good is also important to you.

Emotionally you are fairly stable and you stick by your own standards. Taureans do not respond well to change. Intuition also plays an important part in your life.

Moon in Gemini

You have a warm-hearted character, sympathetic and eager to help others. At times reserved, you can also be articulate and chatty: this is part of the paradox of Gemini, which always brings duplicity to the nature. You are interested in current affairs, have a good intellect and are good company and likely to have many friends. Most of your friends have a high opinion of you and would be ready to defend you should the need arise. However, this is usually unnecessary, as you are quite capable of defending yourself in any verbal confrontation.

Travel is important to your inquisitive mind and you find intellectual stimulus in mixing with people from different cultures. You also gain much from reading, writing and the arts, but you do need plenty of rest and relaxation in order to avoid fatigue.

Moon in Cancer

The Moon in Cancer at the time of birth is a fortunate position as Cancer is the Moon's natural home. This means that the qualities of compassion and understanding given by the Moon are especially enhanced in your nature, and you are friendly and sociable and cope well with emotional pressures. You cherish home and family life, and happily do the domestic tasks. Your surroundings are important to you and you hate squalor and filth. You are likely to have a love of music and poetry.

Your basic character, although at times changeable like the Moon itself, depends on symmetry. You aim to make your surroundings comfortable and harmonious, for yourself and those close to you.

Moon in Leo

The best qualities of the Moon and Leo come together to make you warm-hearted, fair, ambitious and self-confident. With good organisational abilities, you invariably rise to a position of responsibility in your chosen career. This is fortunate as you don't enjoy being an 'also-ran' and would rather be an important part of a small organisation than a menial in a large one.

You should be lucky in love, and happy, provided you put in the effort to make a comfortable home for yourself and those close to you. It is likely that you will have a love of pleasure, sport, music and literature. Life brings you many rewards, most of them as a direct result of your own efforts, although you may be luckier than average and ready to make the best of any situation.

Moon in Virgo

You are endowed with good mental abilities and a keen receptive memory, but you are never ostentatious or pretentious. Naturally quite reserved, you still have many friends, especially of the opposite sex. Marital relationships must be discussed carefully and worked at so that they remain harmonious, as personal attachments can be a problem if you do not give them your full attention.

Talented and persevering, you possess artistic qualities and are a good homemaker. Earning your honours through genuine merit, you work long and hard towards your objectives but show little pride in your achievements. Many short journeys will be undertaken in your life.

Moon in Libra

With the Moon in Libra you are naturally popular and make friends easily. People like you, probably more than you realise, you bring fun to a party and are a natural diplomat. For all its good points, Libra is not the most stable of astrological signs and, as a result, your emotions can be a little unstable too. Therefore, although the Moon in Libra is said to be good for love and marriage, your Sun sign and Rising sign will have an important effect on your emotional and loving qualities.

You must remember to relate to others in your decision-making. Co-operation is crucial because Libra represents the 'balance' of life that can only be achieved through harmonious relationships. Conformity is not easy for you because Libra, an Air sign, likes its independence.

Moon in Scorpio

Some people might call you pushy. In fact, all you really want to do is to live life to the full and protect yourself and your family from the pressures of life. Take care to avoid giving the impression of being sarcastic or impulsive and use your energies wisely and constructively.

You have great courage and you invariably achieve your goals by force of personality and sheer effort. You are fond of mystery and are good at predicting the outcome of situations and events. Travel experiences can be beneficial to you.

You may experience problems if you do not take time to examine your motives in a relationship, and also if you allow jealousy, always a feature of Scorpio, to cloud your judgement.

Moon in Sagittarius

The Moon in Sagittarius helps to make you a generous individual with humanitarian qualities and a kind heart. Restlessness may be intrinsic as your mind is seldom still. Perhaps because of this, you have a need for change that could lead you to several major moves during your adult life. You are not afraid to stand your ground when you know your judgement is right, you speak directly and have good intuition.

At work you are quick, efficient and versatile and so you make an ideal employee. You need work to be intellectually demanding and do not enjoy tedious routines.

In relationships, you anger quickly if faced with stupidity or deception, though you are just as quick to forgive and forget. Emotionally, there are times when your heart rules your head.

Moon in Capricorn

The Moon in Capricorn makes you popular and likely to come into the public eye in some way. The watery Moon is not entirely comfortable in the Earth sign of Capricorn and this may lead to some difficulties in the early years of life. An initial lack of creative ability and indecision must be overcome before the true qualities of patience and perseverance inherent in Capricorn can show through.

You have good administrative ability and are a capable worker, and if you are careful you can accumulate wealth. But you must be cautious and take professional advice in partnerships, as you are open to deception. You may be interested in social or welfare work, which suit your organisational skills and sympathy for others.

Moon in Aquarius

The Moon in Aquarius makes you an active and agreeable person with a friendly, easy-going nature. Sympathetic to the needs of others, you flourish in a laid-back atmosphere. You are broad-minded, fair and open to suggestion, although sometimes you have an unconventional quality which others can find hard to understand.

You are interested in the strange and curious, and in old articles and places. You enjoy trips to these places and gain much from them. Political, scientific and educational work interests you and you might choose a career in science or technology.

Money-wise, you make gains through innovation and concentration and Lunar Aquarians often tackle more than one job at a time. In love you are kind and honest.

Moon in Pisces

You have a kind, sympathetic nature, somewhat retiring at times, but you always take account of others' feelings and help when you can.

Personal relationships may be problematic, but as life goes on you can learn from your experiences and develop a better understanding of yourself and the world around you.

You have a fondness for travel, appreciate beauty and harmony and hate disorder and strife. You may be fond of literature and would make a good writer or speaker yourself. You have a creative imagination and may come across as an incurable romantic. You have strong intuition, maybe bordering on a mediumistic quality, which sets you apart from the mass. You may not be rich in cash terms, but your personal gifts are worth more than gold.

VIRGO IN LOVE

Discover how compatible in love you are with people from the same and other signs of the zodiac. Five stars equals a match made in heaven!

Virgo meets Virgo

Unlike many same-sign combinations this is not a five-star pairing, for one very good reason. Virgo needs to react with other signs to reveal its hidden best side. Two Virgoans together, although enjoying some happiness, will not present a dynamic, sparkling and carefree appearance. They should run an efficient and financially sound household, but that all-important ingredient, passion, may be distinctly low-key. Star rating: ***

Virgo meets Libra

There have been some rare occasions when this match has found great success, but usually the inward-looking Virgoan depresses the naturally gregarious Libran. Libra appears self-confident but is not so beneath the surface and needs encouragement to develop inner confidence, which may not come from Virgo. Constancy can be a problem for Libra, who also tires easily and may find Virgo dull. A less serious approach from Virgo is needed to make this work. Star rating: **

Virgo meets Scorpio

There are one or two potential difficulties here, but there is also a meeting point from which to overcome them. Virgo is very caring and protective, a trait which Scorpio understands and even emulates. Both signs are consistent, but also sarcastic. Scorpio will impress Virgo with its serious side, and may also uncover a hidden passion in Virgo which all too often lies deep within its Earth-sign nature. Material success is very likely, with Virgo taking the lion's share of domestic chores and family responsibilities. Star rating: ***

Virgo meets Sagittarius

There can be some strange happenings in this relationship. Sagittarius and Virgo view life so differently there are always new discoveries. Virgo is much more of a home bird than Sagittarius, but that won't matter if the Archer introduces its hectic social life gradually. More importantly, Sagittarius understands that it takes Virgo a long time to free its hidden 'inner sprite', but once free it will be fun all the way – until Virgo's thrifty nature takes over. There are great possibilities, but effort is required. Star rating: ***

Virgo meets Capricorn

One of the best possible combinations, because Virgo and Capricorn have an instinctive understanding. Both signs know the value of dedicated hard work and apply it equally in a relationship and other areas of life. Two of the most practical signs, nothing is beyond their ken, even if to outsiders they appear rather sterile or lacking in 'oomph'. What matters most is that the individuals are happy, and with so much in common, the likelihood of mutual material success and a shared devotion to home and family, there isn't much doubt of that. Star rating: *****

Virgo meets Aquarius

Aquarius is a strange sign because no matter how well one knows it, it always manages to surprise, and for this reason, against the odds, it's quite likely that Aquarius will form a successful relationship with Virgo. Aquarius is changeable, unpredictable and often quite 'odd' while Virgo is steady, a fuss-pot and very practical. Herein lies the key. What one sign needs, the other provides and that may be the surest recipe for success imaginable. On-lookers may not know why the couple are happy, but they will recognise that this is the case. Star rating: ****

Virgo meets Pisces

This looks an unpromising match from beginning to end. There are exceptions to every rule, particularly where Pisces is concerned, but these two signs are both so deep it's hard to imagine that they could ever find what makes the other tick. Virgo's ruminations are extremely materialistic, while Pisces exists in a world of deep-felt, poorly expressed emotion. Pisces and Virgo might find they don't talk much, so only in a contemplative, almost monastic, match would they ever get on. Still, in a vast zodiac, anything is possible. Star rating: **

Virgo meets Aries

Neither of these signs really understands the other, and that could easily lead to a clash. Virgo is so pedantic, which will drive Aries up the wall, while Aries always wants to be moving on to the next objective before Virgo is even settled with the last one. It will take time for these two to get to know each other, but this is a great business matching. If a personal relationship is seen in these terms then the prognosis can be quite good, but on the whole, this is not an inspiring match. Star rating: ***

Virgo meets Taurus

This is a difficult basis for a successful relationship, and yet it often works. Both signs are from the Earth element, so have a common-sense approach to life. They have a mutual understanding, and share many interests. Taurus understands and copes well with Virgo's fussy nature, while Virgo revels in the Bull's tidy and artistic qualities. Both sides are committed to achieving lasting material success. There won't be fireworks, and the match may lack a certain 'spiritual' feel, but as that works both ways it may not be a problem. Star rating: *****

Virgo meets Gemini

The fact that both these signs are ruled by the planet Mercury might at first seem good but, unfortunately, Mercury works very differently in these signs. Gemini is untidy, flighty, quick, changeable and easily bored, while Virgo is fastidious, steady and constant. If Virgo is willing to accept some anarchy all can be well, but this not usually the case. Virgoans are deep thinkers and may find Gemini a little superficial. This pair can be compatible intellectually, though even this side isn't without its problems. Star rating: ★★★

Virgo meets Cancer

This match has little chance of success, for fairly simple reasons: Cancer's generous affection will be submerged by the Virgoan depths, not because Virgo is uncaring but because it expresses itself so differently. As both signs are naturally quiet, things might become a bit boring. They would be mutually supportive, possibly financially successful and have a very tidy house, but they won't share much sparkle, enthusiasm, risk-taking or passion. If this pair were stranded on a desert island, they might live at different ends of it. Star rating: ★★

Virgo meets Leo

There is a chance for this couple, but it won't be trouble-free. Leo and Virgo view life very differently: Virgo is of a serious nature and struggles to relate to Leo's relentless optimism and cheerfulness and can find it annoying. Leo, meanwhile, may find Virgo stodgy, sometimes dark and uninspiring. The saving grace comes through communication – Leo knows how to make Virgo talk, which is what it needs. If this pair find happiness, though, it may be a case of opposites attract! Star rating: ★★★

VENUS:
THE PLANET OF LOVE

If you look up at the sky around sunset or sunrise you will often see Venus in close attendance to the Sun. It is arguably one of the most beautiful sights of all and there is little wonder that historically it became associated with the goddess of love. But although Venus does play an important part in the way you view love and in the way others see you romantically, this is only one of the spheres of influence that it enjoys in your overall character.

Venus has a part to play in the more cultured side of your life and has much to do with your appreciation of art, literature, music and general creativity. Even the way you look is responsive to the part of the zodiac that Venus occupied at the start of your life, though this fact is also down to your Sun sign and Ascending sign. If, at the time you were born, Venus occupied one of the more gregarious zodiac signs, you will be more likely to wear your heart on your sleeve, as well as to be more attracted to entertainment, social gatherings and good company. If on the other hand Venus occupied a quiet zodiac sign at the time of your birth, you would tend to be more retiring and less willing to shine in public situations.

It's good to know what part the planet Venus plays in your life for it can have a great bearing on the way you appear to the rest of the world and since we all have to mix with others, you can learn to make the very best of what Venus has to offer you.

One of the great complications in the past has always been trying to establish exactly what zodiac position Venus enjoyed when you were born because the planet is notoriously difficult to track. However, we have solved that problem by creating a table that is exclusive to your Sun sign, which you will find on the following page.

Establishing your Venus sign could not be easier. Just look up the year of your birth on the next page and you will see a sign of the Zodiac. This was the sign that Venus occupied in the period covered by your sign in that year. If Venus occupied more than one sign during the period, this is indicated by the date on which the sign changed, and the name of the new sign. For instance, if you were born in 1950, Venus was in Leo until the 10th September, after which time it was in Virgo. If you were born before 10th September your Venus sign is Leo, if you were born on or after 10th September, your Venus sign is Virgo. Once you have established the position of Venus at the time of your birth, you can then look in the pages which follow to see how this has a bearing on your life as a whole.

1920 VIRGO / 5.9 LIBRA
1921 CANCER / 31.8 LEO
1922 LIBRA / 8.9 SCORPIO
1923 LEO / 28.8 VIRGO /
    20.9 LIBRA
1924 CANCER / 9.9 LEO
1925 LIBRA / 16.9 SCORPIO
1926 LEO / 12.9 VIRGO
1927 VIRGO
1928 VIRGO / 5.9 LIBRA
1929 CANCER / 31.8 LEO
1930 LIBRA / 7.9 SCORPIO
1931 LEO / 28.8 VIRGO /
    20.9 LIBRA
1932 CANCER / 9.9 LEO
1933 LIBRA / 16.9 SCORPIO
1934 LEO / 11.9 VIRGO
1935 VIRGO
1936 VIRGO / 4.9 LIBRA
1937 CANCER / 31.8 LEO
1938 LIBRA / 7.9 SCORPIO
1939 LEO / 27.8 VIRGO /
    19.9 LIBRA
1940 CANCER / 9.9 LEO
1941 LIBRA / 15.9 SCORPIO
1942 LEO / 11.9 VIRGO
1943 VIRGO
1944 VIRGO / 4.9 LIBRA
1945 CANCER / 30.8 LEO
1946 LIBRA / 7.9 SCORPIO
1947 LEO / 27.8 VIRGO /
    18.9 LIBRA
1948 CANCER / 9.9 LEO
1949 LIBRA / 15.9 SCORPIO
1950 LEO / 10.9 VIRGO
1951 VIRGO
1952 VIRGO / 3.9 LIBRA
1953 CANCER / 30.8 LEO
1954 LIBRA / 7.9 SCORPIO
1955 LEO / 26.8 VIRGO /
    17.9 LIBRA
1956 CANCER / 8.9 LEO
1957 LIBRA / 15.9 SCORPIO
1958 LEO / 10.9 VIRGO
1959 VIRGO / 20.9 LEO
1960 VIRGO / 3.9 LIBRA
1961 CANCER / 30.8 LEO
1962 LIBRA / 8.9 SCORPIO
1963 LEO / 26.8 VIRGO /
    17.9 LIBRA
1964 CANCER / 8.9 LEO
1965 LIBRA / 15.9 SCORPIO
1966 LEO / 9.9 VIRGO
1967 VIRGO / 10.9 LEO

1968 VIRGO / 2.9 LIBRA
1969 CANCER / 29.8 LEO
1970 LIBRA / 8.9 SCORPIO
1971 LEO / 25.8 VIRGO /
    16.9 LIBRA
1972 CANCER / 8.9 LEO
1973 LIBRA / 14.9 SCORPIO
1974 LEO / 8.9 VIRGO
1975 VIRGO / 3.9 LEO
1976 VIRGO / 2.9 LIBRA
1977 CANCER / 29.8 LEO
1978 LIBRA / 8.9 SCORPIO
1979 VIRGO / 16.9 LIBRA
1980 CANCER / 8.9 LEO
1981 LIBRA / 14.9 SCORPIO
1982 LEO / 7.9 VIRGO
1983 VIRGO / 28.8 LEO
1984 VIRGO / 2.9 LIBRA
1985 CANCER / 28.8 LEO
1986 LIBRA / 8.9 SCORPIO
1987 VIRGO / 15.9 LIBRA
1988 CANCER / 7.9 LEO
1989 LIBRA / 13.9 SCORPIO
1990 LEO / 7.9 VIRGO
1991 LEO
1992 VIRGO / 1.9 LIBRA
1993 CANCER / 28.8 LEO
1994 LIBRA / 8.9 SCORPIO
1995 VIRGO / 15.9 LIBRA
1996 CANCER / 7.9 LEO
1997 LIBRA / 12.9 SCORPIO
1998 LEO / 6.9 VIRGO
1999 LEO
2000 VIRGO / 1.9 LIBRA
2001 CANCER / 28.8 LEO
2002 LIBRA / 8.9 SCORPIO
2003 VIRGO / 15.9 LIBRA
2004 CANCER / 6.9 LEO
2005 LIBRA / 10.9 SCORPIO
2006 LEO / 4.9 VIRGO
2007 LEO
2008 VIRGO / 1.9 LIBRA
2009 CANCER / 28.8 LEO
2010 LIBRA / 8.9 SCORPIO
2011 VIRGO / 15.9 LIBRA
2012 CANCER / 6.9 LEO
2013 LIBRA / 10.9 SCORPIO
2014 LEO / 4.9 VIRGO
2015 LEO
2016 VIRGO / 31.8 LIBRA
2017 CANCER / 28.8 LEO
2018 LIBRA/ 8.9 SCORPIO

VENUS THROUGH THE ZODIAC SIGNS

Venus in Aries

Amongst other things, the position of Venus in Aries indicates a fondness for travel, music and all creative pursuits. Your nature tends to be affectionate and you would try not to create confusion or difficulty for others if it could be avoided. Many people with this planetary position have a great love of the theatre, and mental stimulation is of the greatest importance. Early romantic attachments are common with Venus in Aries, so it is very important to establish a genuine sense of romantic continuity. Early marriage is not recommended, especially if it is based on sympathy. You may give your heart a little too readily on occasions.

Venus in Taurus

You are capable of very deep feelings and your emotions tend to last for a very long time. This makes you a trusting partner and lover, whose constancy is second to none. In life you are precise and careful and always try to do things the right way. Although this means an ordered life, which you are comfortable with, it can also lead you to be rather too fussy for your own good. Despite your pleasant nature, you are very fixed in your opinions and quite able to speak your mind. Others are attracted to you and historical astrologers always quoted this position of Venus as being very fortunate in terms of marriage. However, if you find yourself involved in a failed relationship, it could take you a long time to trust again.

Venus in Gemini

As with all associations related to Gemini, you tend to be quite versatile, anxious for change and intelligent in your dealings with the world at large. You may gain money from more than one source but you are equally good at spending it. There is an inference here that you are a good communicator, via either the written or the spoken word, and you love to be in the company of interesting people. Always on the look-out for culture, you may also be very fond of music, and love to indulge the curious and cultured side of your nature. In romance you tend to have more than one relationship and could find yourself associated with someone who has previously been a friend or even a distant relative.

Venus in Cancer

You often stay close to home because you are very fond of family and enjoy many of your most treasured moments when you are with those you love. Being naturally sympathetic, you will always do anything you can to support those around you, even people you hardly know at all. This charitable side of your nature is your most noticeable trait and is one of the reasons why others are naturally so fond of you. Being receptive and in some cases even psychic, you can see through to the soul of most of those with whom you come into contact. You may not commence too many romantic attachments but when you do give your heart, it tends to be unconditionally.

Venus in Leo

It must become quickly obvious to almost anyone you meet that you are kind, sympathetic and yet determined enough to stand up for anyone or anything that is truly important to you. Bright and sunny, you warm the world with your natural enthusiasm and would rarely do anything to hurt those around you, or at least not intentionally. In romance you are ardent and sincere, though some may find your style just a little overpowering. Gains come through your contacts with other people and this could be especially true with regard to romance, for love and money often come hand in hand for those who were born with Venus in Leo. People claim to understand you, though you are more complex than you seem.

Venus in Virgo

Your nature could well be fairly quiet no matter what your Sun sign might be, though this fact often manifests itself as an inner peace and would not prevent you from being basically sociable. Some delays and even the odd disappointment in love cannot be ruled out with this planetary position, though it's a fact that you will usually find the happiness you look for in the end. Catapulting yourself into romantic entanglements that you know to be rather ill-advised is not sensible, and it would be better to wait before you committed yourself exclusively to any one person. It is the essence of your nature to serve the world at large and through doing so it is possible that you will attract money at some stage in your life.

Venus in Libra

Venus is very comfortable in Libra and bestows upon those people who have this planetary position a particular sort of kindness that is easy to recognise. This is a very good position for all sorts of friendships and also for romantic attachments that usually bring much joy into your life. Few individuals with Venus in Libra would avoid marriage and since you are capable of great depths of love, it is likely that you will find a contented personal life. You like to mix with people of integrity and intelligence but don't take kindly to scruffy surroundings or work that means getting your hands too dirty. Careful speculation, good business dealings and money through marriage all seem fairly likely.

Venus in Scorpio

You are quite open and tend to spend money quite freely, even on those occasions when you don't have very much. Although your intentions are always good, there are times when you get yourself in to the odd scrape and this can be particularly true when it comes to romance, which you may come to late or from a rather unexpected direction. Certainly you have the power to be happy and to make others contented on the way, but you find the odd stumbling block on your journey through life and it could seem that you have to work harder than those around you. As a result of this, you gain a much deeper understanding of the true value of personal happiness than many people ever do, and are likely to achieve true contentment in the end.

Venus in Sagittarius

You are lighthearted, cheerful and always able to see the funny side of any situation. These facts enhance your popularity, which is especially high with members of the opposite sex. You should never have to look too far to find romantic interest in your life, though it is just possible that you might be too willing to commit yourself before you are certain that the person in question is right for you. Part of the problem here extends to other areas of life too. The fact is that you like variety in everything and so can tire of situations that fail to offer it. All the same, if you choose wisely and learn to understand your restless side, then great happiness can be yours.

Venus in Capricorn

The most notable trait that comes from Venus in this position is that it makes you trustworthy and able to take on all sorts of responsibilities in life. People are instinctively fond of you and love you all the more because you are always ready to help those who are in any form of need. Social and business popularity can be yours and there is a magnetic quality to your nature that is particularly attractive in a romantic sense. Anyone who wants a partner for a lover, a spouse and a good friend too would almost certainly look in your direction. Constancy is the hallmark of your nature and unfaithfulness would go right against the grain. You might sometimes be a little too trusting.

Venus in Aquarius

This location of Venus offers a fondness for travel and a desire to try out something new at every possible opportunity. You are extremely easy to get along with and tend to have many friends from varied backgrounds, classes and inclinations. You like to live a distinct sort of life and gain a great deal from moving about, both in a career sense and with regard to your home. It is not out of the question that you could form a romantic attachment to someone who comes from far away or be attracted to a person of a distinctly artistic and original nature. What you cannot stand is jealousy, for you have friends of both sexes and would want to keep things that way.

Venus in Pisces

The first thing people tend to notice about you is your wonderful, warm smile. Being very charitable by nature you will do anything to help others, even if you don't know them well. Much of your life may be spent sorting out situations for other people, but it is very important to feel that you are living for yourself too. In the main, you remain cheerful, and tend to be quite attractive to members of the opposite sex. Where romantic attachments are concerned, you could be drawn to people who are significantly older or younger than yourself or to someone with a unique career or point of view. It might be best for you to avoid marrying whilst you are still very young.

VIRGO:
2017 DIARY PAGES

October
2017

1 SUNDAY
Moon Age Day 11   Moon Sign Aquarius

Not everyone will be on the same wavelength as you are right now and you may have to modify your stance on a number of different issues in order to accommodate others. You could also be facing a puzzle or two today and will have to think long and hard in order to discover the answers you are seeking.

2 MONDAY
Moon Age Day 12   Moon Sign Aquarius

If you need technical assistance today you should not be afraid to ask for it. Even though you are good at most things there are certain jobs that are best left to experts. In a personal sense it looks as though Virgo is brushing off the odd cobweb and dusting down relationships ahead of a much more progressive romantic phase.

3 TUESDAY
Moon Age Day 13   Moon Sign Pisces

This won't turn out to be the most progressive period you have experienced for some time; in fact you may as well stay in bed for all the impact you are going to make on the world at large. This is not to suggest that there are no gains to be made, simply that you shouldn't expect to move any mountains right now.

4 WEDNESDAY
Moon Age Day 14   Moon Sign Pisces

The great thing about the lunar low this month is that although you won't be taking the world by storm, you don't care whether you do or not. Even for hard-working Virgoans there are moments when you need to sit back and take stock. Now is such an interlude and you should relish the opportunity to be more of a watcher.

5 THURSDAY
Moon Age Day 15   Moon Sign Aries

It would be very easy to be distracted today, for example by gossip. Although you will be quite interested to hear the comments from those around you today you should also be wise enough to make up your own mind about all situations. Experience counts for a great deal when you are dealing with professional matters.

6 FRIDAY
Moon Age Day 16   Moon Sign Aries

Be very sure of yourself today before you proceed down any unknown and slightly scary path. This is as true in your social life as it is in a professional sense and you will probably relish the company and support of people you know and trust. For once the recently courageous Virgo is just a little apprehensive.

7 SATURDAY
Moon Age Day 17   Moon Sign Taurus

Standing up for your rights might be slightly more difficult today, mostly because you may not be entirely sure what they are. That's why it is most important to do a little research, to ask the right questions and to read the correct documents. Only when you know the facts of a situation can you move forward and sort it out.

8 SUNDAY
Moon Age Day 18   Moon Sign Taurus

There are significant signs that you are about to undergo a great many changes, though most of these have to do with the way you think and not necessarily with the way you live or work. Virgo begins to open up and to be more honest with itself as well as with other people. Such a metamorphosis can be somewhat uncomfortable.

9 MONDAY
Moon Age Day 19   Moon Sign Taurus

How very jolly you are likely to feel at the moment and just how much happiness you can bring into the lives of those you deal with in a moment-by-moment sense. With more money likely to be coming your way in the near future it looks as though all your hard work in the recent past is now beginning to pay off quite handsomely.

10 TUESDAY
Moon Age Day 20   Moon Sign Gemini

You put on a bold face to the world, even if you are not half as confident as you appear to be. Don't play silly games with people over issues that are far too important to treat lightly and make sure your lover knows exactly how you feel about things. It may be time for a fairly serious heart-to-heart talk.

11 WEDNESDAY
Moon Age Day 21   Moon Sign Gemini

So good is your intuition right now that you won't have any trouble at all working out whether someone is trustworthy or not. The only difficulty could be in convincing others that you are correct. It might eventually be necessary to allow those around you to formulate their own conclusions, whilst you rely heavily on your own gut feelings.

12 THURSDAY
Moon Age Day 22   Moon Sign Cancer

Cool, calm and collected – that's the way Virgo is likely to be just at present. You won't want to push yourself too hard, though you find some interesting shortcuts to success – ones of a sort that wouldn't normally appeal to you. If ever there was a zodiac sign that is ultimately capable of going the long way round it is Virgo.

13 FRIDAY
Moon Age Day 23   Moon Sign Cancer

In most cases if you can visualise it, you can do it. This isn't exclusively true at the moment but when it matters the most your imagination can be a great assistant. Don't get so tied down with Virgo routines that you fail to engage your more dreamy side on occasions. Reach out for something you really want and touch it in your mind.

14 SATURDAY
Moon Age Day 24   Moon Sign Leo

If there is one thing about your nature that almost always remains the same it is your very practical approach to most situations. This can be a tremendous boon to you at present because people around you, especially if you are at work, simply don't have your flair for getting it right first time. Your mechanical skills are particularly good now.

15 SUNDAY
Moon Age Day 25   Moon Sign Leo

It is going to be the personal side of your life that brings out the very best in you this Sunday and you should be keen to find new things to do. You relish the company of people you really like and won't be too keen to mix with strangers or even acquaintances for the moment. This is about to change.

16 MONDAY
Moon Age Day 26   Moon Sign Virgo

The real boost today doesn't so much come from the direction of the lunar high but rather from a mixture of determination and staying power, both of which are well marked at the moment. Very little would cause you to divert from a path you have deliberately and carefully chosen and as is often the case, success is the result.

17 TUESDAY
Moon Age Day 27   Moon Sign Virgo

You can now afford to take a few more chances, though whether you will or not remains to be seen because it isn't your way to gamble too much. Money may come from fairly unexpected sources and you could find yourself significantly better off than you might have expected at this time of the month.

18 WEDNESDAY
Moon Age Day 28   Moon Sign Libra

Today you have a good sense of fun but also perhaps a tendency to act on emotional impulses rather on sound common sense. This won't please you much because as an Earth sign you love to be fully in command of yourself. On the other hand this is something of a holiday for Virgo and perhaps should be treated as such.

19 THURSDAY
Moon Age Day 29   Moon Sign Libra

Career developments are likely to see you with a heightened sense of self-confidence and optimism. It becomes apparent that you are now in the driving seat and that you have what it takes to convince those around you to follow your lead. In a romantic sense especially you are now fully in charge.

20 FRIDAY
Moon Age Day 0   Moon Sign Libra

You might now be inclined to give way to a little mental restlessness but this is a situation you can counter by getting something different and interesting into your life at every possible opportunity. It would be all too easy to get bored or to settle for what you know because it's comfortable. Some effort is necessary but the rewards are great.

21 SATURDAY
Moon Age Day 1   Moon Sign Scorpio

If you feel slightly bored today and in need of a change of scene, do try to avoid being over-impulsive. There are ways and means to make yourself feel more content with your lot and you don't have to turn your entire life upside down. By this evening you will be ready to enjoy your social life.

22 SUNDAY
Moon Age Day 2   Moon Sign Scorpio

Although you are clearly fired up by ambition and should do everything you can to take positive steps towards your dreams, you also need to leave time aside for simple relaxation. At social occasions you should prove to be a hit but you may find yourself associating with people who drive you up the wall.

23 MONDAY
Moon Age Day 3   Moon Sign Sagittarius

The start of a new working week is likely to find you busy and filled with enterprise. Seek out like-minded people because you are especially co-operative now and can formulate successful and long-lasting partnerships. As far as your home life is concerned you might be somewhat agitated by the behaviour of younger people.

24 TUESDAY
Moon Age Day 4   Moon Sign Sagittarius

There are some very subtle influences around at this time so be thoughtful and alert to the nuances of your mood. You may not get quite as much done as you would wish in a concrete sense but your ability to sort things out in your mind has rarely been better. Routines may seem quite comforting at this stage.

25 WEDNESDAY   *Moon Age Day 5   Moon Sign Sagittarius*

In a professional sense it looks as though you will now be able to reap the benefit of all the effort you have been putting in recently. You are certainly likely to be on form and your ideas are interesting to almost anyone who learns about them. One particularly ingenious plan could streamline an otherwise tedious process.

26 THURSDAY   *Moon Age Day 6   Moon Sign Capricorn*

Your social life is likely to be happy and stimulating at this time. You tend to meet interesting and dynamic people and you have much to offer. Don't allow your idea of your own limitations to hold you back in any situation or let your natural modesty get in the way of a very big idea. You have an eye for the main chance and should also be lucky now.

27 FRIDAY   *Moon Age Day 7   Moon Sign Capricorn*

This is a time when you need to gain approval, not because you doubt your own reasoning but merely for the sake of your own self-esteem. In a way it is a low-key way of blowing your own trumpet, but there is nothing at all wrong with that. People should be pleased to confirm your conclusions and will find you warm and friendly.

28 SATURDAY   *Moon Age Day 8   Moon Sign Aquarius*

Your social life is likely to expand this weekend and although it is relatively easy for you to get things done in a practical sense it is more likely that you will be drawn into having fun. This would be a good time in which to broaden your experiences through travel but if you don't have the time to go wandering physically, you can do so in your head.

29 SUNDAY   *Moon Age Day 9   Moon Sign Aquarius*

Peace and quiet at home probably won't be much of an option today. It will seem as though there is always some situation or another that is demanding your attention and there could also be a great deal of noise and commotion around. As a result you might decide it would be better to go somewhere else, though the noise will probably go with you.

30 MONDAY
Moon Age Day 10   Moon Sign Pisces

Life could so easily turn out to be a series of misunderstandings whilst the lunar low is around and if you want to avoid these you are going to have to explain yourself carefully on numerous occasions. All of this holds you up slightly and can be quite frustrating but forewarned is forearmed and arguments can be circumvented.

31 TUESDAY
Moon Age Day 11   Moon Sign Pisces

Whatever you take on board today, be aware that your level of energy is not high and that common good luck doesn't really favour your efforts now. For these reasons it might be best to watch and wait while you allow others to make most of the running. At least personal attachments should be unaffected by the lunar low.

November
2017

1 WEDNESDAY
Moon Age Day 12   Moon Sign Pisces

You may discover that you are now more ambitious, probably because of events that have taken place across the last week or so. A position that you never expected to hold could well be in the offing and general trends show that you begin to have more confidence in your ability to get ahead in life than has been the case for a while.

2 THURSDAY
Moon Age Day 13   Moon Sign Aries

Professional success is likely to come naturally, even if you find yourself fending off individuals who are extremely competitive. You make your way forward slowly, steadily and with great panache, whereas those around you are more likely to struggle. People will admire your cool and efficient way of getting things done.

3 FRIDAY
Moon Age Day 14   Moon Sign Aries

Wherever practical initiatives are concerned you may find information relating to projects that are becoming ever more important to you. This is a time to lead from the front and to convince others that you really know what you are talking about. Expect some good results from your efforts and enlist the support of colleagues.

4 SATURDAY
Moon Age Day 15   Moon Sign Taurus

It is probably not a good idea to believe everything you hear today. For one thing your informants have probably got hold of the wrong end of the stick and for another they may have a vested interest in telling a tale in a particular way. It would be better by far to receive a couple of unbiased accounts and then to make up your own mind.

5 SUNDAY
Moon Age Day 16   Moon Sign Taurus

Domestic and family ties benefit from present planetary trends and you will be getting on especially well with younger people. It seems that you are presently very good at putting yourself in the other person's shoes, no matter how different those might be to your own. People appreciate your ability to listen quietly and offer sound advice.

6 MONDAY
Moon Age Day 17   Moon Sign Gemini

You need to allow your personality to shine out today because that's all it takes to impress those around you. Things should be better on the romantic front and that means you may be spending a loving period with that most special person. Some friends can be quite distant today – and not in terms of miles.

7 TUESDAY
Moon Age Day 18   Moon Sign Gemini

Virgo could now be rather too idealistic for its own good. It's fine to have beliefs and to follow them as much as you can but there are moments when a greater degree of flexibility proves to be necessary in the real world. You have to remember that not everyone's values and opinions are going to be the same as yours.

8 WEDNESDAY
Moon Age Day 19   Moon Sign Cancer

Although practical matters can prove to be quite tiresome today you do realise that they have to be dealt with and nobody is better at addressing them than you are. More imagination could be called for later in the day and it looks as though you are going to have to be very flexible in your dealings with errant family members.

9 THURSDAY
Moon Age Day 20   Moon Sign Cancer

Although there are likely to be some misunderstandings to deal with today, in the main you manage to sort these out quite easily and won't be held up much by anything. You see your way forward quite clearly and though you may not be taking too many practical steps today your mind is set on positive actions for later.

10 FRIDAY
Moon Age Day 21   Moon Sign Leo

It looks as though you will become assertive and even forceful for the moment. That's fine just as long as you don't allow things to get out of hand. A little humility along the way is also important, if only because it shows other people that you are keeping your feet on the ground. New friendships are likely around now.

11 SATURDAY
Moon Age Day 22   Moon Sign Leo

Being in the know can make a big difference when it comes to achieving successes and that is why it would be most sensible to keep your ear to the ground today. Even the most casual remarks can offer you invaluable clues and once you take these on board you are half way to achieving some notable coups, especially at work.

12 SUNDAY
Moon Age Day 23   Moon Sign Virgo

There is now a real emphasis on making money and you will be doing all you can to increase the amount coming into your purse or pocket. With some very ingenious ideas at your disposal you should also be in a good position to work out strategies for the future, even years ahead, that will keep the cash rolling in.

13 MONDAY
Moon Age Day 24   Moon Sign Virgo

You show a very cheerful and tolerant attitude towards almost everyone and will be popular, as much for what you are giving out as for any other reason. Virgo can be a quiet sign sometimes but that doesn't appear to be the case at present because you seem to be the life and soul of the party.

14 TUESDAY
Moon Age Day 25   Moon Sign Libra

This is a marvellous time to reaffirm your identity and to make sure that everyone knows who you are and what you want. In fact you can be a variety of different individuals today, dependent on what you are doing. In each case it is important to show yourself in the best possible light to the maximum number of people.

15 WEDNESDAY *Moon Age Day 26   Moon Sign Libra*

Virgo is normally very careful and that certainly seems to be true today. No matter how much other people push you will only do what seems right and sensible to you personally. In the main that's fine because your friends know you well but you may have to make a few exceptions in the case of new acquaintances or strangers.

16 THURSDAY *Moon Age Day 27   Moon Sign Libra*

You will now be more gregarious and extremely generous to those you care about. To counter this somewhat you won't be inclined to give anything away to people you don't know or who you find difficult to trust. Virgo can be very partisan on occasions and this is now more likely than ever. Details matter to you at this time.

17 FRIDAY *Moon Age Day 28   Moon Sign Scorpio*

It is clear that you will benefit from being out of doors and in places with wide horizons. Your confidence remains generally high but there may be moments when you are more inclined to doubt yourself, especially if things start to go wrong. Keep faith with your original opinions and methods and don't change horses in midstream.

18 SATURDAY *Moon Age Day 0   Moon Sign Scorpio*

Don't take too many risks this weekend and if you are regularly involved in sporting activities you need to be especially careful for the moment. It isn't that anything is likely to go very wrong but you are not quite as co-ordinated as you usually are. People generally are likely to seem duller than usual – or is that your own attitude?

19 SUNDAY *Moon Age Day 1   Moon Sign Sagittarius*

You can rid your life of a few nonessentials now and start some new trends. Get together with a trusted individual and start working on new strategies that have been playing around in your head for a while. There are some gains to be made today from showing how inspirational you can be, particularly when it comes to romance.

20 MONDAY   *Moon Age Day 2   Moon Sign Sagittarius*

If there are problems regarding joint finances around now you need to sit down and talk things through, rather than keeping silent and hoping everything will come good in the end. It might also be sensible to reassess your attachments to certain possessions. Are you benefiting from them or working just to maintain them?

21 TUESDAY   *Moon Age Day 3   Moon Sign Sagittarius*

You should fit quite well into almost any slot today and that is because you are making yourself so adaptable. It doesn't matter much what company you keep because you change like a chameleon in order to suit your environment – a fact that isn't lost on those around you. In romance you are considerate, caring and, in the eyes of someone, sexy.

22 WEDNESDAY   *Moon Age Day 4   Moon Sign Capricorn*

You tend to personify self-sacrifice today because you will go so far in order to make those around you happy. To do so will seem more important than feathering your own nest, though if you are wise you can achieve both objectives at the same time. You may be adopting a new attitude with regard to family matters.

23 THURSDAY   *Moon Age Day 5   Moon Sign Capricorn*

You now begin to develop a deeply analytical approach to quite a few matters, which is typical of Virgo. Your practical skills are certainly on display and you may be able to sort out a mess caused by others. There is no doubt that you are the right person to call upon for assistance. Watch how many people realise this.

24 FRIDAY   *Moon Age Day 6   Moon Sign Aquarius*

Given the right social circumstances and a responsive crowd you can give a good account of yourself at the moment, even if the underlying trend is for you to be fairly quiet for most of the time. You have a strong need for reassurance, especially in your work, and you won't approach anything new unless you are very sure of yourself.

25 SATURDAY
Moon Age Day 7   Moon Sign Aquarius

A wonderful boost to your social life comes along now and the weekend ought to work out somewhat better than you may have expected. This is because you are in the mood to entertain and also on account of the sort of people who are gathering around you at this time. Today is not a period for working too hard or for worrying.

26 SUNDAY
Moon Age Day 8   Moon Sign Aquarius

Someone is likely to challenge you today, or else make statements with which you definitely do not agree. Whether or not you do anything about the situation depends on how strongly you feel about it. The chances are that for the moment you will keep your counsel. But heaven help anyone who crosses you in any way tomorrow.

27 MONDAY
Moon Age Day 9   Moon Sign Pisces

Whatever you decide is right for today – go for it Virgo. Don't let anyone tell you what you should be thinking or doing and use the lunar high to the best of your ability in every practical sense. This is not the sort of day to wait in a queue or to stand around wondering whether you should move or not. Keep friends laughing all day.

28 TUESDAY
Moon Age Day 10   Moon Sign Pisces

Another good day is in store, though today probably won't be quite as eventful as yesterday. What the lunar high leaves you right now is a strong sense of purpose, a desire to enjoy yourself and a great deal of affection for those around you. All of these are positive ingredients for a Tuesday that can be filled with joy and happiness.

29 WEDNESDAY
Moon Age Day 11   Moon Sign Aries

Your natural sensitivity is well emphasised and you tend to be more of a shrinking violet today – unless you are dealing with matters you understand absolutely. Finding the level of confidence you need to make big changes is going to be hard, which is why you tend to nibble away at the edge of things.

30 THURSDAY   *Moon Age Day 12   Moon Sign Aries*

There is now a possibility that you will express yourself somewhat vaguely and you are unlikely to take sufficient time out to work out what you should be saying. When it matters the most and you are dealing with someone you love deeply, words probably won't be important in any case – a simple look may be enough.

December

2017

1 FRIDAY
Moon Age Day 13   Moon Sign Taurus

It's almost as if you can fly at present because you seem to have a bird's eye view of life. You can see when people are doing things badly – or when they are not doing them at all, and you know very well when people could do with a hand. Once you have such an understanding it ought to be simple to lend a timely helping hand.

2 SATURDAY
Moon Age Day 14   Moon Sign Taurus

Being part of a team is likely to work out for the best for you today. Although you are quite single-minded as a rule you will now have a greater willingness to see another point of view, even when it is radically different from your own. Somewhere there is someone who could be of great help to you today. Your job is to find out just who it is.

3 SUNDAY
☿ *Moon Age Day 15   Moon Sign Gemini*

Your sensitivity increases and you are apt to be in a fairly dreamy state. This might cause you to think about the past and to become slightly nostalgic. The fact that Christmas is not far ahead won't help this tendency, though of course there is nothing at all wrong with enjoying a few happy memories – perhaps try to share them?

4 MONDAY
☿ *Moon Age Day 16   Moon Sign Gemini*

Your love life could put a little strain on matters at the start of this week. Maybe you are just not feeling amorous or it could be that your partner is slightly difficult to deal with at the moment. One way or another you are far more likely to mix freely with a number of different people and to leave the deeper emotions for another day.

5 TUESDAY ☿ *Moon Age Day 17 Moon Sign Cancer*

Though personal relationships could be slightly low-key at this stage, you will get on well with just about everyone. You feel the need to share your affection around and may not be in the mood to make a special fuss of any one individual. Some new starts you make today could seem too slow but it won't take you long to gain speed.

6 WEDNESDAY ☿ *Moon Age Day 18 Moon Sign Cancer*

You now find yourself more expressive and well able to communicate with just about anyone you come across. Not all your efforts to help others will work out strictly as you might have expected and there could be the odd disappointment on the way. In the main you will be happiest at the moment when the pace of life is extremely fast.

7 THURSDAY ☿ *Moon Age Day 19 Moon Sign Leo*

There are lots of communications to deal with now and also quite possibly a feeling that you would like to spend more time in and around your home. When you are dealing with practical matters it is important to do things your own way and not to get bogged down by the rather strange ideas of others. Virgo usually knows what to do.

8 FRIDAY ☿ *Moon Age Day 20 Moon Sign Leo*

A dilemma of some sort is likely to arise in relationships. Find a balance between acting upon your own personal needs and the requirements that others have of you. If there are any problems today these could arise as a result of a misunderstanding and not for any solid or serious reason. Things can be talked through easily enough.

9 SATURDAY ☿ *Moon Age Day 21 Moon Sign Virgo*

You seem to thrive on a challenge at present and will be facing most situations head on today. There is very little that is now beyond your capabilities and the lunar high also makes you much luckier and inclined to succeed at most things first time. When Virgo is in this frame of mind nobody is inclined to argue.

10 SUNDAY ☿ *Moon Age Day 22   Moon Sign Virgo*

You continue to make things happen, both inside and outside of work. What is also significant is the fact that your popularity is about as high as it can get. That means you are flavour of the month, even to people you don't normally get on with too well. You should also expect to be doing rather well in the financial stakes.

11 MONDAY ☿ *Moon Age Day 23   Moon Sign Virgo*

Your ideas are good and definitely make sense, not only to you but also to colleagues and friends. Don't keep things to yourself, especially when it is something that has been on your mind for weeks. It's time to break the mould as far as Virgo is concerned and to show everyone just how amazing you can be.

12 TUESDAY ☿ *Moon Age Day 24   Moon Sign Libra*

Opportunities come along to improve your lot in and around your home. It should now be easier to listen to relatives who have been having a slightly difficult time and to implement plans that can help. Time stretches like elastic for Virgo at this stage of the week and you will be amazed at just how much you can achieve.

13 WEDNESDAY ☿ *Moon Age Day 25   Moon Sign Libra*

Communication remains especially important and it is within your social interactions that your greatest joys come at the moment. It may be occurring to you for the first time just how close it is to Christmas but being the sort of person you are you won't panic. Rather you will sit down and make a plan for yourself.

14 THURSDAY ☿ *Moon Age Day 26   Moon Sign Scorpio*

You are unlikely to be making snap decisions today but will be thinking things through very carefully indeed. That's your way and though it doesn't always impress other people, you can't avoid this side of your nature. It looks as though you will be showing ever more concern for certain individuals who are worse off than you are.

15 FRIDAY ☿ *Moon Age Day 27   Moon Sign Scorpio*

Money matters can be quite complex to deal with and when they involve your partner or the family as a whole you might decide that a meeting of minds is called for. You are unlikely to take draconian actions of any sort at this time and can be guaranteed to show a fair and even-handed attitude to almost any situation.

16 SATURDAY ☿ *Moon Age Day 28   Moon Sign Scorpio*

Communication with influential people could prove to be worth a good deal to you at this time and it seems as though you come across interesting types all the time. If you are at work you might have to stand up for your rights more than usual – that is if you don't want colleagues to be either stealing your thunder or else using your ideas.

17 SUNDAY ☿ *Moon Age Day 29   Moon Sign Sagittarius*

What a great time this is likely to be for pleasant social relationships. Maybe it's the onset of the festive season but more likely it is the planetary influences that surround you. For whatever reason you become more open and can even make the running in most situations. Don't leave important little details of any sort to chance.

18 MONDAY ☿ *Moon Age Day 0   Moon Sign Sagittarius*

There's no doubt that today works better for you if you concentrate on a specific task rather than trying to get everything done at the same time. There's a bit of a dichotomy today because although you want to have everything straight and logical, rules and regulations are inclined to get on your nerves. Make careful moves.

19 TUESDAY ☿ *Moon Age Day 1   Moon Sign Capricorn*

You like to manifest yourself and your talents in a truly original way and you could also be making use of some of the gifts that come to you at present. This would be a good time to travel, maybe to see family members or friends, though some Virgos could even be utilising this time to take a fantastic holiday.

20 WEDNESDAY ☿ *Moon Age Day 2   Moon Sign Capricorn*

Money, property and possessions will all play an important part in your thinking in this part of December. You see new opportunities picked out as if they were underlined and you can't understand why everyone isn't as dynamic and go-getting as you presently are. Make allowances for a colleague or a friend with real problems.

21 THURSDAY ☿ *Moon Age Day 3   Moon Sign Capricorn*

Circumstances might seem to conspire to irritate you today, especially at work. There are a few troublesome planets about at the moment as far as you are concerned but none are malevolent. Take things in your stride and don't react to circumstances you cannot alter. Later in the day you are likely to feel somewhat less frazzled.

22 FRIDAY ☿ *Moon Age Day 4   Moon Sign Aquarius*

Your real forte now lies in communication, which isn't always the case for Virgo. You will also enjoy anything mentally stimulating and intellectual. If you decide on an outing today it would be good to go somewhere that gets you thinking and creative. Pleasing your lover should be easier now than at any stage.

23 SATURDAY *Moon Age Day 5   Moon Sign Aquarius*

This could be a more relaxing day, though of course it all depends on family commitments because some Virgoans could be up until the early hours wrapping those last-minute presents. In the main you will choose to have fun and can do much to lift the spirits of everyone around you. For once Virgo is a true optimist.

24 SUNDAY *Moon Age Day 6   Moon Sign Pisces*

Today can bring you face-to-face with consequences, especially if you make rash decisions whilst the lunar low is around. It would be far better for the moment to defer making up your mind until you feel more certain of your position. Friends should prove to be very supportive and you may be inclined to rely on them.

25 MONDAY
Moon Age Day 7   Moon Sign Pisces

You may feel a little reluctant to become involved in matters that you would have grasped with both hands last week, but don't panic because this is a very temporary state of affairs. This might be a slightly muted Christmas Day in some respects but you should feel generally safe, secure and very loved.

26 TUESDAY
Moon Age Day 8   Moon Sign Pisces

Getting out and about is more likely from tomorrow on and left to your own devices you might be quite happy to stay around your own fireside for the moment. Of course that might not be possible but do at least try to take part of the day to relax. You also have a growing and quite perceptible desire to solve puzzles of one sort or another.

27 WEDNESDAY
Moon Age Day 9   Moon Sign Aries

If there are obstacles in your path today you need to carry on regardless of them. There are times at the moment when standard responses won't work and that's where your present ingenuity comes in. Get together with people you don't see much during the year and make the most of social encounters to further your own ideas.

28 THURSDAY
Moon Age Day 10   Moon Sign Aries

It would be far too easy right now to come across as somewhat self-centred and although this isn't really the case, try to show a little humility to convince others. Your concern is not simply for yourself but on behalf of those who are important in your life. The only problem could be that they fail to realise it.

29 FRIDAY
Moon Age Day 11   Moon Sign Taurus

Lots of your energy is piled equally into work and play around now and there is a balance to your life that should be pleasing you no end. You are not that far away from completing something that could seem to be a real chore and with the end of one phase will come the potential start of another. It's time to start planning well ahead.

30 SATURDAY   *Moon Age Day 12   Moon Sign Taurus*

It seems to be your technical know-how that helps you to get on at work or at home and there isn't any doubt that specialist skills are worth most to you today. Concentrate on those things you know that others don't because people are likely to be relying heavily on you. You can shine like a star in all social settings both today and for New Year.

31 SUNDAY   *Moon Age Day 13   Moon Sign Gemini*

This may be the best day of the whole Christmas period for get-togethers and for meeting up with people you really love but who you don't spend time with very often. Whilst others make hopeful resolutions for the year ahead, you remain confident that you have everything in place to ensure your continued success.

VIRGO:
2018 DIARY PAGES

VIRGO:
YOUR YEAR IN BRIEF

It is likely that the start of 2018 will be a time of ups and downs. January and February offer new commitments, especially when it comes to romance, and you could also be making new friends and influencing people at work. If you are in full time education the first two months of the year are likely to be extremely positive for you. Family members give you every reason to be proud of the efforts they are making and old debts could be repaid.

Although this time has its slight problems March and April should find you in the mood for some fun, although get important jobs out of the way first. People from the past are likely to enter your life again, together with a special new friendship that is likely to be developing at this time. Conversations are important now, since they fire you with enthusiasm and force you to think about things that have been delayed.

May brings many changes of fortune, which by June should become the greatest optimism you have enjoyed for a while. Build your plans steadily and think ahead. This is especially true if you are beginning a new relationship, which will work better in the long run if you don't put too much pressure on the other party. Allow people to come round to your ideas slowly, and once they do, there is every chance your plans will be the ones they follow.

You can afford to push your luck a little during July and August. This really is a good period for Virgo to chance its arm in a number of different ways. At this time you could be making career changes, moving about more than usual, and also making significant alterations with regard to your home. With a lot of confidence, what you ask for you tend to get.

September and October are probably the only two months of the year during which you are keeping a lower profile, so expect things to slow down a little. It isn't that you fail to get anything done, more that you are willing to watch and wait. This is a good thing because it is close to the end of the year that you can benefit the most by putting carefully laid plans into action. Hold off some of them until the beginning of November

Allow your personality to shine through November and December and light up the world like at no other time throughout this year. You have so much to offer but you too often allow circumstances and people to get in your way. This is a period to really show what you are capable of achieving. Christmas should lots of fun, but take care to avoid exhaustion.

January

2018

1 MONDAY
Moon Age Day 14   Moon Sign Gemini

As the year begins you may feel a strong yearning to search for new discoveries. You love travel now and would do well to make a move in some direction if it proves to be possible and you certainly will not gain a great deal by staying in the same place and waiting for life to come to you.

2 TUESDAY
Moon Age Day 15   Moon Sign Cancer

At this time you are at your very best when you are sticking up for your convictions. There are several planetary influences around now that show you as being forthright and determined. Although Virgo is often a fairly quiet zodiac sign, there are occasions when you will fight like a tiger for what you believe.

3 WEDNESDAY
Moon Age Day 16   Moon Sign Cancer

This would be a really good time to exploit the possibility of a change of scenery. There is a sort of restlessness about you now that cannot be dealt with by simply doing the same old things. You need to see new places and to experience different ways of looking at old problems. Take a friend and just go somewhere.

4 THURSDAY
Moon Age Day 17   Moon Sign Leo

Financial prospects look reasonably good and could improve enormously if you take the right actions at the right time. There isn't much room for mistakes at the moment but if you use a combination of common sense and intuition you should not go far wrong. This is a time of skilful manoeuvring for most Virgos.

5 FRIDAY
Moon Age Day 18   Moon Sign Leo

When it comes to sorting out your career you should be filled with vitality and replete with the sort of good ideas that can take you a long way. Your mind tends to be very inventive at the moment and even the simplest idea that comes into your head could easily be turned to your advantage. Listen to the advice of a good friend.

6 SATURDAY
Moon Age Day 19   Moon Sign Virgo

You should expect the best today and in the main you will be able to get it. Don't settle for something less than you want and be willing to charm others in order to get them to follow your lead. There is great good luck around and you should discover that you are better off than you expected to be financially.

7 SUNDAY
Moon Age Day 20   Moon Sign Virgo

Your thinking, ideas and philosophies now tend to be quite original and even unique in some way. This makes you very attractive to most of the people you meet, even if one or two of them have some doubts about your ideas. Look out for a journey you haven't taken before, even if it is only an excursion in your mind.

8 MONDAY
Moon Age Day 21   Moon Sign Libra

Don't let ideas languish just because you might be feeling slightly unsure about your own capabilities. You are much more dextrous and clever than you believe yourself to be and the only commodity you might lack around now is confidence. There are occasions when you will simply have to jump into the water, no matter what.

9 TUESDAY
Moon Age Day 22   Moon Sign Libra

You possess the will to win, but do you have everything in place in order to do so? Look at life again and make sure that you have dealt with every eventuality before you proceed. As long as you know you have covered your back around people you don't trust, you can move forward into an entirely different and potentially successful zone.

10 WEDNESDAY   *Moon Age Day 23   Moon Sign Scorpio*

Though your life is likely to be quite positive on a material plane, sometimes things come so easily to you at present that you don't appreciate what is yours for the taking. Be willing to enjoy what you achieve and don't look ahead so far that you fail to realise what is good in your life now. Support your friends today.

11 THURSDAY   *Moon Age Day 24   Moon Sign Scorpio*

The planetary focus is now on money and finances generally. This would be a good time for getting a loan or for signing documents that demand a good understanding of the small print. Avoid family arguments and wherever it proves to be possible be open and honest. Not everyone wants to agree with you under present trends.

12 FRIDAY   *Moon Age Day 25   Moon Sign Scorpio*

In a professional sense there is a slight danger that you may be putting in so much effort that you are going to burn yourself out. The weekend lies just around the corner and for some Virgoans it ought to start today. Stand back and allow others to make some of the running. Watching and waiting is a part of what you are about.

13 SATURDAY   *Moon Age Day 26   Moon Sign Sagittarius*

Your love life and social matters are both well highlighted under the major trends for this weekend. It's true that you may not have what it takes to feather your nest in a professional sense, but instead you have been given everything you need to make yourself popular and to help everyone around you enjoy what is going on.

14 SUNDAY   *Moon Age Day 27   Moon Sign Sagittarius*

You tend to shine in professional matters, though of course this cannot apply unless you are actually at work today. For those who can call Sunday their own, there is some useful planning to be done and you should also find you have enough time to make a big fuss of family members. Don't get obsessed with details right now.

15 MONDAY   *Moon Age Day 28   Moon Sign Capricorn*

You can afford to be more expansive in your thinking. Don't push your mind down paths you already know well but rather opt for new modes of thinking. The more you seek, the greater will be the rewards that come your way. Avoid getting depressed about situations that you cannot alter no matter what you try to do about them.

16 TUESDAY   *Moon Age Day 0   Moon Sign Capricorn*

Perhaps you are now feeling more creative and expressive than has been the case recently. If so, cater for these trends by taking on something new and by finding new ways to communicate to the world at large. People you haven't seen for quite some time are now likely to appear in your life again – like a bolt from the blue.

17 WEDNESDAY   *Moon Age Day 1   Moon Sign Capricorn*

Conversations you have with others are likely to have a profound part to play in the way you are thinking and could cause you to make the odd u-turn. Don't worry if you have to change a few plans because what you are doing is repositioning yourself in the light of changing circumstances. Get onside with friends who have big ideas.

18 THURSDAY   *Moon Age Day 2   Moon Sign Aquarius*

You can now get all the usual benefits from your home, whilst at the same time introducing a little excitement into the place. If there are family members who have ideas for renovation or redecoration in the house, listen carefully to what they have to say. Co-operative ventures work well now and never better than in a domestic setting.

19 FRIDAY   *Moon Age Day 3   Moon Sign Aquarius*

A sense of personal triumph and a big boost to your ego can be expected around now. It seems as though you are doing everything right, though as always pride can go before a fall so some care is still necessary. You have a great sense of what looks right at the moment and will want to present yourself in the best possible way.

20 SATURDAY   *Moon Age Day 4   Moon Sign Pisces*

Look out for obstacles in your everyday life and don't get too upset when they come along. For you the lunar low works best when you are happy to rely on the help and good offices of friends and colleagues. You do plenty for others and nobody will mind taking some of the strain for you. After all, it's only for a short while.

21 SUNDAY   *Moon Age Day 5   Moon Sign Pisces*

Your approach to certain events in your social and personal life is likely to be somewhat hesitant and pessimistic. The short-term restrictions you are feeling at the moment are simply the result of the monthly lunar low. Keep an open mind but don't take any chances. It's best to know where you stand.

22 MONDAY   *Moon Age Day 6   Moon Sign Pisces*

If you are looking for backing from others you may have to ask for it. Don't expect things to fall in your lap at the moment and be prepared to put in extra effort, especially in social matters. Love looks better and there is a strong sense of romance around you this week. It is in this direction that you are most likely to be looking.

23 TUESDAY   *Moon Age Day 7   Moon Sign Aries*

A break from everyday routine is called for, as you remain basically restless and inclined to look for fresh fields and pastures new. That's fine for today but won't be so likely tomorrow. If there are new incentives to deal with at work, so much the better but prepare yourself for a slightly quieter period at home.

24 WEDNESDAY   *Moon Age Day 8   Moon Sign Aries*

It is just possible today that you will put your own desires ahead of those of other people in your immediate circle. It isn't like Virgo to be selfish, but you may feel that what you want will also benefit those around you. If that's genuinely the case then why not proceed? You will need the courage of your convictions, not just today but for weeks to come.

25 THURSDAY
Moon Age Day 9   Moon Sign Taurus

You now have a very natural sense of the best way to communicate with others and you show a very positive face to the world of work during this part of the week. Those Virgoans who are in full time education should be getting on especially well, even if circumstances force some sort of change on you that you might wonder about.

26 FRIDAY
Moon Age Day 10   Moon Sign Taurus

Now you have a great deal of emotional energy and it shouldn't be difficult to tell your partner exactly how you feel about them. Channel your efforts in sensible directions and leave airy-fairy schemes to other people. You will always instinctively know if a particular course of action is really worth following.

27 SATURDAY
Moon Age Day 11   Moon Sign Gemini

Inspirational and personal success is yours for the taking, even if the going seems a little difficult at first today. It's quite likely you will be away from work right now and in all probability you will be planning your next moves, rather than putting them into action. Loved ones should be quite attentive now.

28 SUNDAY
Moon Age Day 12   Moon Sign Gemini

At the moment you make friends easily and can add significantly to your social life by joining groups or organisations that haven't been a part of your life in the past. There are plenty of choices to be made, in some ways too many for conservative Virgo. Before you fully commit yourself to anything it might be best to stop and think.

29 MONDAY
Moon Age Day 13   Moon Sign Cancer

An emotional matter is likely to demand your attention on this particular Monday but if you don't feel all that qualified to make a judgement, watch and wait. This is not a good time to become involved in arguments and it would be far better to let others disagree, rather than to get yourself into situations that won't help you at all.

30 TUESDAY *Moon Age Day 14   Moon Sign Cancer*

When it comes to career developments you should be at your best right now but you will need to rely on the good offices of those around you. This should not be difficult because you are generally very popular and people actively want to lend you a hand. Beware the onset of complicated situations at home.

31 WEDNESDAY *Moon Age Day 15   Moon Sign Leo*

Good rewards come from the direction of your social life, not to mention your love life, which looks especially good at the present time. This is a period during which you should do your best to have fun, without having to think too much about the practicalities of life. For that reason it would be good to get out of the house.

♍ February 2018

1 THURSDAY
Moon Age Day 16   Moon Sign Leo

You will have the opportunity to step into the limelight today and should be sure to take advantage of the situation. There are planetary influences about right now that make you good to have around and everyone clamours for your attention. Now is the time to ask for something you really want.

2 FRIDAY
Moon Age Day 17   Moon Sign Virgo

Newer and better opportunities come your way now, thanks to the arrival of the lunar high. With a greater level of physical energy and a determination that is going off the scale, this is the time to get what you want from life. Routines are definitely not for you on this particular day and you will want to make some sweeping changes.

3 SATURDAY
Moon Age Day 18   Moon Sign Virgo

Your confidence is not lacking now and it's absolutely essential that you do whatever you can to get ahead whilst the astrological trends are so good. Standard responses to situations won't work and you need to show how ingenious you can be. Thinking on your feet will be no difficulty today.

4 SUNDAY
Moon Age Day 19   Moon Sign Libra

You have a communicative and friendly attitude today and should be quite happy to mix freely with all sorts of people. The caring and sharing side of Virgo is clearly on display and you have what it takes to bring others round to your specific point of view. Romance is also favoured under present trends.

5 MONDAY
Moon Age Day 20   Moon Sign Libra

It's possible that you could become a little irritated when dealing with others, though of course this won't include everyone. The sort of person you want to avoid is the kind who has to be told a dozen times but still won't do things the way you want. It would be better to leave them to their own devices for now.

6 TUESDAY
Moon Age Day 21   Moon Sign Libra

Most social interaction tends to be informative at present and will offer you new opportunities that can mature in the fullness of time. There's no doubt about your present ingenuity, or your ability to make a silk purse from a sow's ear. Individuality is the name of the game and you have it in bucket-loads today.

7 WEDNESDAY
Moon Age Day 22   Moon Sign Scorpio

Stand by for a restless period during which you should engage as much as possible in new ideas, in order to get the very most out of life. A few words in the right direction could pep up your romantic life no end, whilst Virgos who have been looking for love of late may well prove luckier around this time.

8 THURSDAY
Moon Age Day 23   Moon Sign Scorpio

Much of your energy at this time is likely to be going into group activities and there isn't much doubt that you are up for a good time. People you don't see very often are likely to return to your life around now and should bring with them some new opportunities and ideas that mean plenty of fun in the near future.

9 FRIDAY
Moon Age Day 24   Moon Sign Sagittarius

Others may not be prepared for you to be quite as assertive as you are at the moment. As a result they may be shocked and more likely to automatically fall in line with your wishes. There's nothing remotely negative about Virgo under present astrological trends and you know exactly what you want.

10 SATURDAY   *Moon Age Day 25   Moon Sign Sagittarius*

You are likely to be very innovative this weekend and know well how to further your intentions. The silliest ideas can become practical realities and you should not turn away from any idea that pops into your head without at least looking at it carefully. Don't get too bogged down with minor details.

11 SUNDAY   *Moon Age Day 26   Moon Sign Sagittarius*

This would be a good time to try out some of your new ideas on other people. There is a strong need for compromise, especially in personal attachments. Listen to what your partner is saying and even if you don't entirely agree, go along with their thinking. The last thing you need to be today is a bulldozer.

12 MONDAY   *Moon Age Day 27   Moon Sign Capricorn*

Capitalise on all the potential within yourself and do whatever proves to be necessary to get ahead. A series of better planetary trends have arisen which make it easier to make and hold on to money. Don't forget birthdays or anniversaries and make a real fuss of someone in the family who has scored a success.

13 TUESDAY   *Moon Age Day 28   Moon Sign Capricorn*

Complications are now possible and these come in the main from a slight inability on your part to see someone else's point of view. Loved ones need especially careful handling at this juncture and you won't get anywhere if you try to impose your views on them, particularly younger family members.

14 WEDNESDAY   *Moon Age Day 29   Moon Sign Aquarius*

This is a wonderful time to expand your social interests and to take some time out to simply enjoy yourself. This might mean having to delegate but there should be at least a few people you can rely on. All work and no play can make Virgo a dull boy or girl, but some diversion peps you up no end.

15 THURSDAY   *Moon Age Day 0   Moon Sign Aquarius*

Due to increased enthusiasm, energetic initiative and the ability to cope under professional pressure, you should get on extremely well today. You can make an especially good impression on people in charge and there isn't much doubt about the fact that people are watching you with great respect around this time.

16 FRIDAY   *Moon Age Day 1   Moon Sign Aquarius*

You remain very keen to be accommodating and to help out those around you as much as you possibly can. On a less favourable note you have a tendency to dig your heels in right now, sometimes regarding issues that are of little real importance. Try to be as flexible as possible and to laugh off unimportant obstacles.

17 SATURDAY   *Moon Age Day 2   Moon Sign Pisces*

Although there are likely to be a few setbacks with regard to specific plans, in the main you cope very well with the quieter interlude in which you find yourself. It isn't hard for Virgo to be slightly withdrawn and the situation even has its advantages. For one thing the world leaves you alone to think.

18 SUNDAY   *Moon Age Day 3   Moon Sign Pisces*

A few minor problems are likely to surface around now – probably ones associated in some way with your family or perhaps a very close friend. You will want to do everything you can to lend a hand but might be prevented from doing so by particular issues. Don't let matters get any more complicated than they have to be.

19 MONDAY   *Moon Age Day 4   Moon Sign Aries*

This is likely to be a promising period in the career department or in education if that's where you spend your days at the moment. The lunar low has passed and it becomes easier to pay attention to what is going on in the world around you. Even casual comments from others are certain to make you happy.

20 TUESDAY
Moon Age Day 5   Moon Sign Aries

Focus on what needs bringing to the surface as far as your love life is concerned and don't get too preoccupied with matters that are of no real consequence. Show how much you understand your partner and to be willing to listen to something they have to say, even if it seems irrelevant to you.

21 WEDNESDAY
Moon Age Day 6   Moon Sign Taurus

Whatever you want to achieve in the longer term is likely to feature heavily on your mind around this time. You are putting in that extra bit of effort that can make all the difference and you show a very positive face to the world in a general sense. Things may not seem quite so straightforward later in the week.

22 THURSDAY
Moon Age Day 7   Moon Sign Taurus

Take care not to push yourself any more than is necessary and stick to what you know instead of going off at a tangent. It's true that others might seem to be getting ahead and you won't have the answers you require at any given moment. However, you remain good to know and should be quite satisfied with your present lot.

23 FRIDAY
Moon Age Day 8   Moon Sign Taurus

What is really important at the moment is to be able to put yourself in the shoes of other people. Fortunately, this is something you find easy to do right now and your strong empathy shines out like a star. It may take you some time to explain something to a person who has difficulty with new things but your patience will win out.

24 SATURDAY
Moon Age Day 9   Moon Sign Gemini

Most social matters should be quite harmonious and where there may have been differences of opinion between yourself and other family members, these are now likely to be sorted out. Today's trends are great for teamwork and for building a new platform from which you can operate more efficiently in the future.

25 SUNDAY
Moon Age Day 10   Moon Sign Gemini

Some relationships could feel as though they are slightly more trouble than they are worth, especially if you constantly have to put yourself out for a so-called friend who seems to do nothing but insult you. There are new social possibilities on the way and it may be that you have simply outgrown one or two relationships from the past.

26 MONDAY
Moon Age Day 11   Moon Sign Cancer

From a social point of view this should be a busy period and you may also discover that your love life is improving – even if you seem to have done little or nothing to promote the change. Keep up your efforts to streamline something at work but try not to make yourself unpopular if people think you are working too hard.

27 TUESDAY
Moon Age Day 12   Moon Sign Cancer

If life throws you into the path of someone you really admire, make the most of the situation, and don't shy away. You have every right to be involved with them. On a personal level you are much more talented than you believe and you might even get the chance to prove it at some stage during today.

28 WEDNESDAY
Moon Age Day 13   Moon Sign Leo

You seem to be filled with emotional drive today and it is towards relationships at every level that you are likely to turn your attention. Before the day is very old you should be forming new attachments that might at first seem casual but some of them could prove to be more important later. Money matters seem quite settled now.

2018

1 THURSDAY
Moon Age Day 14   Moon Sign Leo

Friendships can be absorbing today and it would pay to invest in social relationships that have a practical side to them. Some Virgoans will now be getting involved in keep fit routines or dietary regimes of one sort or another. This is not unusual for you in early spring and it has a great deal to do with your gradually improving self-esteem.

2 FRIDAY
Moon Age Day 15   Moon Sign Virgo

This is a time when a new decisive approach will be more than worthwhile. You won't be able to hang back, even if you would like to do so. The lunar high does make demands of you but these are easy enough to fulfil when energy levels are so high. Rely on your intuition even more than usual and act quickly.

3 SATURDAY
Moon Age Day 16   Moon Sign Virgo

Now is the time to step out into the world and to become even more active. It doesn't matter which area of your life you are dealing with, the approach is likely to be the same. The weekend offers new opportunities to enjoy yourself, while at the same time you find ways to make things better in a personal and a financial sense.

4 SUNDAY
Moon Age Day 17   Moon Sign Libra

There could be good rewards in the offing in terms of social gatherings at this time. Keep your eyes open for the chance to get ahead through the intervention of friends and it is likely that you will be on top form when it comes to small investments or calculated risks. New hobbies are also likely at this time.

5 MONDAY
Moon Age Day 18   Moon Sign Libra

The time is now right to follow your heart and this will also mean speaking your mind when emotional issues come to the fore. Virgo could be slightly quieter than usual in some respects, which makes it somewhat more difficult to get your message across. Your confidence might take a knock but you can bounce back immediately.

6 TUESDAY
Moon Age Day 19   Moon Sign Scorpio

Family members need more tolerance than usual and this is certainly going to be the case where younger people are concerned. If you are a mature Virgo you might have to cast your mind back to the way you behaved when you were young. It won't take long for you to see things from another point of view and to react accordingly.

7 WEDNESDAY
Moon Age Day 20   Moon Sign Scorpio

You know how to get the best out of family members and friends and you are also likely to be even more attentive than usual when it comes to pleasing your partner. This is probably not a day for taking too much on in a practical sense, mainly because you want to be close to those you care about and to enjoy your home surroundings.

8 THURSDAY
Moon Age Day 21   Moon Sign Sagittarius

Social and co-operative ventures are highlighted and the planetary picture favours new adventures. The year is moving on and you won't be inspired if you have to stay indoors all the time. Try to ring the changes and to get some fresh air at some stage today. Even a walk in the park would be better than nothing.

9 FRIDAY
Moon Age Day 22   Moon Sign Sagittarius

You can't please all of the people all of the time and this is especially true in your home setting. Do what you think is right and everything should fall into place. There are moments today when you will want to be quiet and to contemplate your next actions. By tomorrow everything will move more quickly and be far more stimulating.

10 SATURDAY   *Moon Age Day 23   Moon Sign Sagittarius*

You might have to look fairly closely at apparent problems within existing relationships, though these could turn out to be of little importance. As is often the case you take something that doesn't really deserve your attention and worry about it needlessly. Try to concentrate instead on issues that really do have some significance.

11 SUNDAY   *Moon Age Day 24   Moon Sign Capricorn*

You are entering a restless streak and a large part of your mind is constantly asking questions about the way the world works. All this curiosity could find you delving into regions you have avoided before. Keep abreast of news and things that are happening in your back yard and show an interest in social changes.

12 MONDAY   *Moon Age Day 25   Moon Sign Capricorn*

It is highly likely that someone fairly close to you will be acting in a way that seems deliberately intended to annoy you. This is almost certainly not the case but you will be more inclined to take offence at present than would usually be the case. Avoid reacting too strongly to anything at this part of the month.

13 TUESDAY   *Moon Age Day 26   Moon Sign Aquarius*

Slight mishaps are possible at home if you don't pay attention to what you are doing. It also looks as though you would be far better off today taking complete control of your own life because those around you have little idea of what really suits you. If you take matters into your own hands you also need to be tactful towards others.

14 WEDNESDAY   *Moon Age Day 27   Moon Sign Aquarius*

When it comes to sorting out the kind of details that might sometimes make you squirm you are now second to none. Not only are you good at dealing with the minutiae of your own life, you can also do it for your partner and close friends. People love to have you around and especially so when you are so kind and attentive.

15 THURSDAY   *Moon Age Day 28   Moon Sign Aquarius*

It may seem as if outside influences are conspiring to make life more awkward but all you are really looking at is your own attitude. If you stay basically optimistic, yet don't expect too much to be going your way, what follows is likely to be moderate contentment. Stand up for friends today but don't get involved in heated discussions.

16 FRIDAY   *Moon Age Day 29   Moon Sign Pisces*

Anything that is clearly not succeeding in your life, despite your best efforts, probably needs altering or leaving behind. While the lunar low is around you can be quite ruthless in terms of what you are willing to discard. Don't get too tied up with the problems of others but be on hand to at least listen to them. In most cases that is enough.

17 SATURDAY   *Moon Age Day 0   Moon Sign Pisces*

Pressing emotional issues could get in the way of the practical side of your life and this is fairly typical of what happens to Virgo when the lunar low arrives. Your mind can easily become muddled and you just don't see things as clearly as you usually would. If you don't know what to do – don't do anything.

18 SUNDAY   *Moon Age Day 1   Moon Sign Aries*

In social relationships today you could be getting yourself at odds with friends and even family members. There appears to be a distinct difference between the way you want to proceed and the ideas that those around you have. Some extra diplomacy is called for but don't rely on the assumption that people will come good, even if they agree at first.

19 MONDAY   *Moon Age Day 2   Moon Sign Aries*

Self-confidence in professional matters is really important this week and even if you don't have much it is worth behaving as if you do. If people think you know what you are doing they will place more responsibility on your shoulders. You can work out how to deal with it later but for now just act as if you know everything.

20 TUESDAY
Moon Age Day 3   Moon Sign Aries

The need to put your personal input into life is now very strong and there isn't too much point in waiting around for other people to have all the good ideas. On the contrary you would be much better off following the dictates of your own mind, even when you have to persuade everyone around you that you know best.

21 WEDNESDAY
Moon Age Day 4   Moon Sign Taurus

Trends suggest that friends and colleagues might prove to be distinctly unreliable and it won't be easy to persuade them around to your point of view. If people don't trust your opinions as much as usual, this might be because you are not entirely sure of yourself. The more confident you appear, the better things go.

22 THURSDAY
Moon Age Day 5   Moon Sign Taurus

This is another good time to push ahead with practical plans. In contrast to yesterday, planetary influences now inspire you with confidence and you won't be at all hesitant when it comes to putting your name forward for anything. You could find it slightly difficult to put aside your own wishes for the sake of those around you.

23 FRIDAY
☿ *Moon Age Day 6   Moon Sign Gemini*

Take care that anything you undertake today is not at the expense of someone else. You can be a little too focused in your desires under present trends so look carefully at all possibilities before you embark upon them. If you fail to do so you could irritate someone, and that's something you don't need.

24 SATURDAY
☿ *Moon Age Day 7   Moon Sign Gemini*

Some social situations could prove to be tense and you display a certain mental restlessness as you go about your daily life. Your temper is likely to be shorter than usual and situations you would normally shrug off may easily irritate you. The good thing is that if you are prepared for this trend, you can also deal with it.

25 SUNDAY ☿ *Moon Age Day 8   Moon Sign Cancer*

Your imagination tends to be quite highly developed at this time. On one level that's fine because it means you can think through strategies with flexibility. On the other hand, you could find yourself worrying about things that haven't happened and which probably won't. It's a case of using a planetary trend in a sensible manner.

26 MONDAY ☿ *Moon Age Day 9   Moon Sign Cancer*

What you learn in a professional situation can stand you in good stead for later on, which is why it is now so important to keep your eyes and ears open. On a personal footing you are really sensitive to the needs of your partner and can make them feel like the most special person in the world without much effort.

27 TUESDAY ☿ *Moon Age Day 10   Moon Sign Leo*

Don't get so immersed in your own world that you fail to realise how things look from an entirely different point of view. Keeping your mind occupied is important but it needs to be with thoughts that have practical applications in the wider world. For now you need to be social and gregarious, which suits you and those around you.

28 WEDNESDAY ☿ *Moon Age Day 11   Moon Sign Leo*

You should now be well on top of most financial matters and could even discover a way of earning money that hasn't been a part of your thinking in the past. Perhaps you are looking at some sort of part time job or gaining as a result of moves and ideas that you had some time ago. It's time to use all your initiative.

29 THURSDAY ☿ *Moon Age Day 12   Moon Sign Virgo*

The time is right to follow your intuition, no matter where it might seem to be leading you. The lunar high brings you masses of confidence and a knowing knack of getting things right first time. Put some energy into making dreams into realities and also make the most of the improving weather and the chance to travel.

30 FRIDAY   ☿   *Moon Age Day 13   Moon Sign Virgo*

This may be the best day of the month for getting new projects going. Good luck is on your side and what is even more important is that you are able to take opportunities and make them work well for you. It isn't simply a case of believing in yourself because other people will be trusting you and also offering their support.

31 SATURDAY   ☿   *Moon Age Day 14   Moon Sign Libra*

The feeling of belonging to a group is now quite important and you will find that you work much better when you can co-operate. A friend's advice about a business opportunity could be worth listening to and you are altogether more confident now when you know that there is a strong approval coming from colleagues.

April

2018

1 SUNDAY ☿ *Moon Age Day 15 Moon Sign Libra*

You may be required to consider some adjustments around now, especially in the way you view your career. There are gains to be made but some of these will not be immediately obvious and might even look at first like obstacles. There are times in social situations when you must go with the flow.

2 MONDAY ☿ *Moon Age Day 16 Moon Sign Scorpio*

Be careful about giving away personal information, especially to people you don't instinctively trust. In the main you can rely on your intuition, which is quite sound and reliable at this time. It is the case that not everyone believes what you are saying but you need to retain the courage of your convictions.

3 TUESDAY ☿ *Moon Age Day 17 Moon Sign Scorpio*

There isn't much doubt that you are a sharp thinker at the moment and it is highly unlikely that anyone could make a fool of you. All the same it would be best to check and double-check what you are told before you take it as being the entire truth. Some of the people you meet today could have their own agendas.

4 WEDNESDAY ☿ *Moon Age Day 18 Moon Sign Scorpio*

Challenges in your daily life are now going to reach a peak and there are likely to be issues to deal with that will take up your time and which might stop you in your tracks. You could also experience some delays due to what you see as being pointless rules and regulations. That famous Virgo patience is now very important.

5 THURSDAY   ☿ *Moon Age Day 19*   *Moon Sign Sagittarius*

Getting your own way at this time is largely a matter of using your charm. You can persuade other people to do more or less what you want and there ought to be no shortage of happy interludes coming your way. Present planetary positions can cause financial glitches but make you extremely good to know.

6 FRIDAY   ☿ *Moon Age Day 20*   *Moon Sign Sagittarius*

You now have great confidence in yourself, but what really stands out under present trends is your need to do something different and to see places you don't already know well. If you get the chance to make any sort of journey today, grab it with both hands. An underlying need for excitement cannot be ignored.

7 SATURDAY   ☿ *Moon Age Day 21*   *Moon Sign Capricorn*

The chances are that you are feeling especially unselfish this weekend, which is one reason why so much of your time is likely to be given over to helping others in one way or another. The only reward you are likely to seek is the knowledge that you have done some good. Don't be surprised if people tell you today how wonderful you are.

8 SUNDAY   ☿ *Moon Age Day 22*   *Moon Sign Capricorn*

Things may not be quite what they seem when it comes to affairs of the heart. The more you talk to your partner today, the better you will understand exactly how their mind is working. It's important to be realistic right now and to avoid the sort of wishful thinking that seems good but actually achieves nothing at all.

9 MONDAY   ☿ *Moon Age Day 23*   *Moon Sign Capricorn*

This is hardly the best time of the month for careful, detailed effort of the sort you usually love. For now you want to look at the broad spectrum of life and you won't be at all interested in the nuances. Standard responses to family members probably won't work and if you want to keep everyone happy today you will need to be ingenious.

10 TUESDAY ☿ *Moon Age Day 24   Moon Sign Aquarius*

Today there are people around who will do everything they can to take advantage of you. What makes matters slightly worse is that some of these people are very close to you. We all become slightly selfish at one time or another and all you have to do is to have a quiet word in a few ears and make your own position quite plain.

11 WEDNESDAY ☿ *Moon Age Day 25   Moon Sign Aquarius*

Your personal life is now best described as inconsistent. It isn't that you care any less than you normally do but it may not be easy to put your feelings into words just now. You could also be on a go-slow policy when it comes to jobs you usually do with ease at home. People could find you a little grumpy.

12 THURSDAY ☿ *Moon Age Day 26   Moon Sign Pisces*

Things are likely to slow somewhat but the lunar low will be of relatively little importance this month. All that you are likely to notice is that you can't get ahead quite as fast as you would wish. Meanwhile, you should find that your love life is working out extremely well and that you have plenty of optimism.

13 FRIDAY ☿ *Moon Age Day 27   Moon Sign Pisces*

Once again there are restrictions, but nothing you find especially awkward to deal with. It could be that you will have some difficulty making the advances you would wish at work and not everyone seems to be on your side. Look out for someone who is saying one thing to you but something different to others.

14 SATURDAY ☿ *Moon Age Day 28   Moon Sign Pisces*

Anxieties regarding relationships are probably not important, even if they seem to be at first. If you have doubts it would be best to have a quiet word and to establish what is really going on. The chances are that you are worrying without any just cause but that is something that Virgo is inclined to do now and again.

15 SUNDAY   *Moon Age Day 29   Moon Sign Aries*

Your thoughts and your way of communicating are both imbued with more than a little intuition today and this is something you should be willing to rely upon. Keep up the good work when it comes to moving forward in any sporting endeavours but try to co-operate, rather than competing. Sharing works well but selfishness is counter-productive.

16 MONDAY   *Moon Age Day 0   Moon Sign Aries*

Be careful at the beginning of this week because a professional issue could cause a rather tense atmosphere unless you take it by the scruff of the neck and deal with it immediately. Be direct in all your dealings right now because hedging your bets won't work. Friends display some confidence in you.

17 TUESDAY   *Moon Age Day 1   Moon Sign Taurus*

Take professional issues in your stride, proving once again how reliable you are, even when under some small stress. You can't expect everyone to agree with your point of view at the moment but in the end you will invariably turn out to be right. People should listen to Virgo more than they do and for today at least they will.

18 WEDNESDAY   *Moon Age Day 2   Moon Sign Taurus*

Keep your counsel and avoid getting involved in arguments that belong to others. It's all too easy today to pass an opinion on almost any subject, but it won't necessarily do you any good. Be willing to leave specific subjects to people who are experts in their own field. It would be unfortunate if anyone accused you of being a know-it-all.

19 THURSDAY   *Moon Age Day 3   Moon Sign Gemini*

Because of your willingness to give – to be supportive and to show empathy at the moment, you are generally very popular. Someone might decide that you deserve a treat because of what you have done for them and even if this is only a string of compliments it will do your ego no end of good. Romance looks good for a few days, probably starting today.

20 FRIDAY   *Moon Age Day 4   Moon Sign Gemini*

Keep a tight hold on your purse strings for now and don't speculate too much regarding matters you do not fully understand. Of course you could make it your business to find out what is really happening and then you would be in a better position to take a financial chance. On the whole you may decide to save money.

21 SATURDAY   *Moon Age Day 5   Moon Sign Cancer*

Don't be at all surprised if there are new and interesting people entering your life around now. The Moon in particular makes you curious at the moment and you want to know what makes everyone, even strangers, tick. The fact that you are interested promotes discussion and this in turn could lead to new friendships being formed.

22 SUNDAY   *Moon Age Day 6   Moon Sign Cancer*

Take full advantage of better circumstances in terms of finances and make the most of new opportunities to get ahead. Some good news should be coming in regarding money, perhaps as a result of actions you took in the past. Friends have confidences to impart and one or two of these could prove to be especially surprising.

23 MONDAY   *Moon Age Day 7   Moon Sign Leo*

You will enjoy being the centre of attention wherever you go today. It would be a shame if the planetary aspects creating this tendency were wasted, simply because this was nothing more than a routine day. Put yourself out to make sure there are social possibilities after work and utilise them.

24 TUESDAY   *Moon Age Day 8   Moon Sign Leo*

It appears that having fun is likely to be your number one priority on this Tuesday. Although this is somewhat difficult in the midst of a busy life, you do presently have the ability to mix business with pleasure and to enjoy them both. Look for people who haven't been around recently and take the chance to have a chat.

25 WEDNESDAY   *Moon Age Day 9   Moon Sign Virgo*

Now the possibilities should become obvious and with the lunar high around you have everything necessary to make progress in most spheres of your life. With extra luck on your side you can afford to take a few more chances and you should soon see that colleagues and friends are working for you.

26 THURSDAY   *Moon Age Day 10   Moon Sign Virgo*

Just as was the case yesterday, this is a great time to start new projects and to show the world what you are capable of achieving. It may be necessary to go it alone on occasions because not everyone is as adventurous as you will be. Any risks you take tend to be calculated ones and in the main you know exactly what you are doing.

27 FRIDAY   *Moon Age Day 11   Moon Sign Virgo*

The good times continue. You are now in a very good position to call the shots where future plans are concerned. What matters is that you are doing your homework, which others may not manage so well. This means your point of view is reasoned and difficult to fault. In business, you tend to be extremely shrewd at present.

28 SATURDAY   *Moon Age Day 12   Moon Sign Libra*

The more widespread and different the company you find yourself in today, the better you are likely to feel. Abandoning for the moment thoughts of security and comfort, you may be seeking to put yourself to the test in a physical sense. Remember birthdays in the family and amongst your friends. This is a good emailing day.

29 SUNDAY   *Moon Age Day 13   Moon Sign Libra*

A short interlude shows that today is definitely one of those times during which you get out of life almost exactly what you put into it. If you want to be lethargic, situations won't demand much of you, but you won't make the gains either. Better by far to go for gold and then to revel in the attention that comes your way.

30 MONDAY   *Moon Age Day 14   Moon Sign Scorpio*

It looks as though you won't have time for personal indulgences and will be tied up for much of the day with one issue or another. If you can break away, focus some thinking on a personal desire or aspiration. The more you feel you are moving forward, the more this feels like a positive period.

May

2018

1 TUESDAY
Moon Age Day 15   Moon Sign Scorpio

Today's trends make you a dominant personality. It isn't as if you are the noisiest person around but in your cool and even calculating way and using clever psychology, you can get what you want from others, most of whom would not dream of arguing with you at the moment.

2 WEDNESDAY
Moon Age Day 16   Moon Sign Sagittarius

Prepare to enjoy some success at work, partly because you are so likeable and even charismatic at the moment. People instantly recognise your abilities so don't be surprised if extra responsibility is coming your way. A few distractions are likely but these merely serve to spice up your non-working hours.

3 THURSDAY
Moon Age Day 17   Moon Sign Sagittarius

The tempo of everyday life is likely to speed up now. You move quickly and efficiently towards your objectives and on the way you will discover how much fun life can be. Mixing business with pleasure is definitely your forte around now and you should not turn down any invitation that sounds interesting and potentially rewarding.

4 FRIDAY
Moon Age Day 18   Moon Sign Sagittarius

With improved self-respect you should have little difficulty making good progress, especially where your work is concerned. You may also be getting more involved with community projects and putting some energy towards making your immediate environment more comfortable for everyone you know.

5 SATURDAY   *Moon Age Day 19   Moon Sign Capricorn*

Now is a time to re-evaluate your ideas and to look again at issues that might have been something of a trial to you across the last few weeks. You will have new ways of dealing with old situations and you should also be quite definite in your desire to travel more and to learn about the world. Friends want to be on board with your plans.

6 SUNDAY   *Moon Age Day 20   Moon Sign Capricorn*

Much of the increased energy you have at the moment is likely to be given over to play rather than to work. That's fine because Virgo is no different from any other sign when it comes to a need for enjoyment. Don't only look at what you can gain today but rather how much you enjoy what you are managing to achieve.

7 MONDAY   *Moon Age Day 21   Moon Sign Aquarius*

By taking care of emotional matters you are storing up brownie points for later. If your partner is out of sorts or worried about something, now is the time to get to grips with it and to sort it out fully. At work you may be gaining speed but there are likely to be some people around who seem to be quite obstructive.

8 TUESDAY   *Moon Age Day 22   Moon Sign Aquarius*

Love and romance come easily to Virgo at this time and you should find it easy to please your partner – or even to find one if you are presently single. In all sorts of ways it is important to keep your eyes open because there are opportunities about that should not be missed. Trust your innate judgement at work.

9 WEDNESDAY   *Moon Age Day 23   Moon Sign Aquarius*

Today should bring opportunities for increased success on a practical level and you will be very capable in your thinking and actions today. If at all possible, get out of the house and enjoy the wide world beyond your own door. Horizons need to be broadened and the early summer offers the chance.

10 THURSDAY   *Moon Age Day 24   Moon Sign Pisces*

Trying too hard to succeed is not to be recommended today or tomorrow. You would be better advised to settle for what you have and to plan ahead, rather than pushing and pushing towards some fairly mythical objective. The lunar low prevents you from realising your full potential and even makes you somewhat negative too.

11 FRIDAY   *Moon Age Day 25   Moon Sign Pisces*

Things may seem heavy and onerous at work and you won't have the level of energy necessary to get situations going your way. Why try? For now simply let others make the running, sit back and take a well-earned rest. All the issues will still be there tomorrow and by that time you will be on top form again.

12 SATURDAY   *Moon Age Day 26   Moon Sign Aries*

Right now there are happy influences about and social matters look better than your working life. That is not to suggest you are failing in any professional way, merely that you find the greatest joy when there is fun to be had. Don't be too inclined to see obstacles where personal attachments are concerned because these can be overcome.

13 SUNDAY   *Moon Age Day 27   Moon Sign Aries*

Now is a time for hogging the limelight. All leisure and social activities look good and you should be quite positive in your thinking. Newer and better ways of dealing with old situations may occur to you and there is scope for advancement in your work. At the end of the day, give yourself over to relaxation and fun.

14 MONDAY   *Moon Age Day 28   Moon Sign Taurus*

At work it looks as though you will definitely be in control and you have what it takes to develop new strategies and to work positively towards whatever objectives are on your mind. Although it is only the start of the week you are likely to be planning for next weekend and will be laying down a few ground rules already.

15 TUESDAY   *Moon Age Day 0   Moon Sign Taurus*

What a wonderful period this would be for parties or in fact any sort of gathering at which you find yourself amongst friends. You can be right up there at the centre of things and your sometimes-reserved nature is now exploding with possibilities and general chatter. Most important of all, you are happy inside yourself.

16 WEDNESDAY   *Moon Age Day 1   Moon Sign Gemini*

You may have little time for life's pleasures today as obligations get in the way. Because you are going to be such a busy Virgo it might be good to look at offers of help that might be on the table at this time. In relationships, keep a sense of proportion and avoid over-reacting to silly situations.

17 THURSDAY   *Moon Age Day 2   Moon Sign Gemini*

Take care because there are certain issues that are coming to a head on this, a day when it counts to be careful. You can't avoid them, even though intense concentration on the practical really isn't easy at this stage. It ought to be possible for you to have the best of both worlds. The emphasis in the evening should be on romance.

18 FRIDAY   *Moon Age Day 3   Moon Sign Cancer*

Being out in the social mainstream is fun now. What matters the most to you is your ability to make a good impression on the world at large. This ought to be especially true at work, where it seems likely you will be influencing the decisions of people far from your own personal responsibility. If you don't work today, go shopping instead.

19 SATURDAY   *Moon Age Day 4   Moon Sign Cancer*

You are in a nostalgic mood today and are inclined to spend quite a lot of time looking back to the past, more so than focusing on what is happening in the here and now. As you are also feeling fairly secure with your lot in life you should be worrying less about matters of personal security.

20 SUNDAY
Moon Age Day 5   Moon Sign Leo

Consider taking a break and a holiday around now if at all possible. You deserve a rest and a bit of genuine relaxation, which will be difficult to find during your normal, daily routine. The more you can get away from business or vocational matters, the greater is the chance that you will genuinely ring the changes.

21 MONDAY
Moon Age Day 6   Moon Sign Leo

Think about a little expansion in terms of your home surroundings. Perhaps you need more space and although you may not be able to move house in order to get what you need, a little reorganisation might do the trick. It's time to get to grips with domestic issues that have actually been on your mind for quite some time now.

22 TUESDAY
Moon Age Day 7   Moon Sign Leo

Today you should be most content with things taking place in groups. There are some times when Virgo prefers to go it alone. After all, you can't guarantee that others will do things properly! But at the moment this is less important because you have a strong influence on the way those around you will behave.

23 WEDNESDAY
Moon Age Day 8   Moon Sign Virgo

Getting your own way with just about anyone should be a piece of cake while the lunar high is around. The present position of the Moon brings a real boost to your energy levels and potentially to your ego too. You have a very positive way of putting things across to others that means they are almost certain to agree with you.

24 THURSDAY
Moon Age Day 9   Moon Sign Virgo

This would be the best of times to be thinking about starting a new job, or else getting to grips with issues that have been bothering you for a while. Your potential for work is very good and you are physically stronger than usual. Sporting activities could well appeal to you and any sort of challenge will be looked at positively.

25 FRIDAY   *Moon Age Day 10   Moon Sign Libra*

You can get a good uplift from your personal and romantic life and should not spend so much time doing practical things at present that you fail to take into account the needs of your heart. In particular you want others, or especially one other, to tell you how wonderful you are. Be aware that a little fishing might be necessary.

26 SATURDAY   *Moon Age Day 11   Moon Sign Libra*

You may feel as though you have a great need to hold on to your finances at the moment, though in reality this is probably not the case. You are usually very much in charge of your life in this sense and it is unlikely that you will relax your grip under present trends. Some slight worries regarding family members are just possible.

27 SUNDAY   *Moon Age Day 12   Moon Sign Scorpio*

Although your romantic and social life might now seem to be in a state of some flux, out of the confusion can come something bigger and better. It may seem at times during Sunday that people are not really listening to what you have to say. Nothing could be further from the truth, as you should soon discover.

28 MONDAY   *Moon Age Day 13   Moon Sign Scorpio*

All your efforts in the competitive world are utilised in a positive and successful way. You have a knowing knack of getting things right first time. This is something that those around you are inclined to notice and they will be very supportive of your efforts. Look for change today. Maybe you should embark on a shopping spree?

29 TUESDAY   *Moon Age Day 14   Moon Sign Sagittarius*

Avoid allowing ambitious ideas to dominate your personality. There is a time and a place for showing how positive you can be but also moments when the undoubted sensitivity of your sign will come to the fore. Domestic matters should prove to be more high-spirited than ever at this stage of the week.

30 WEDNESDAY   *Moon Age Day 15   Moon Sign Sagittarius*

It is possible that you will find yourself in a rather taxing role as a result of demands in your career, particularly at this stage of the week. There will be people around who would be more than willing to offer you some timely advice but it isn't at all certain that you want to listen. Virgo can be more than a little stubborn at this time.

31 THURSDAY   *Moon Age Day 16   Moon Sign Sagittarius*

A fairly lucrative financial period is likely now. There is scope for more forward progress and it is easier to get on with those around you than will have been the case recently. A boost to practical matters could well come from family members or friends who have especially good ideas.

June

2018

1 FRIDAY
Moon Age Day 17   Moon Sign Capricorn

You will have little patience when it comes to making compromises at present. In most circumstances this won't cause a problem. You know what you want and will be unlikely to make life difficult for others as a result. It is likely that you are feeling lacking in energy at present and this shows in many areas of your life.

2 SATURDAY
Moon Age Day 18   Moon Sign Capricorn

It seems as though this is going to be an especially good period for advancing new ideas. You can easily handle several different matters at the same time and should be more than willing to take on challenges that have worried you in the past. Stand by a friend who really needs your support at present.

3 SUNDAY
Moon Age Day 19   Moon Sign Aquarius

Domestic matters look as though they are likely to be the most rewarding area of life today, though that doesn't mean that you should diminish your efforts to get in on the commercial world too. In many respects this is almost certainly going to be a fairly routine sort of day, though nonetheless useful for that.

4 MONDAY
Moon Age Day 20   Moon Sign Aquarius

Leisure pursuits will be less rewarding today than practical jobs. That means that you are in efficient mode and at least a few family members could find this trend more difficult to deal with than you do. Make a good time better by slowing down the pace in the evening and do take notice of loved ones.

5 TUESDAY
Moon Age Day 21   Moon Sign Aquarius

You are in the thick of things work-wise now, even if you are retired or between positions at present. The fact is that you want something to do and you are unlikely to stay still for very long. This attracts attention, not least of all from the direction of some people you find to be very attractive.

6 WEDNESDAY
Moon Age Day 22   Moon Sign Pisces

If it suddenly appears that everyone is getting on better in life than you are, you can blame the arrival of the lunar low. Pitching yourself against specific tasks is probably not to be recommended right now and it would be better to find something quiet to do, or else to spend your time looking ahead and planning your next move.

7 THURSDAY
Moon Age Day 23   Moon Sign Pisces

The planetary go-slow continues and there is little you can do about it. Fortunately you come from a patient part of the zodiac and you don't necessarily need to be on the go all the time. Look for a little luxury. You work hard enough generally and so can probably afford to cosset yourself now.

8 FRIDAY
Moon Age Day 24   Moon Sign Aries

There is likely to be some hopeful news arriving regarding your personal concerns and wishes, so keep your eyes and ears open today. Above all you need a change to everyday routines and travel is definitely on the cards for at least some Virgo-born people right now. Keep your options open.

9 SATURDAY
Moon Age Day 25   Moon Sign Aries

Along comes a period that appears to be one of considerable personal gain. Professional matters are also catered for by the present position of the Moon. Firm up your life and notice where the best trends are operating. Shrewd and active, it appears that you know exactly how to make things go your way.

10 SUNDAY
Moon Age Day 26   Moon Sign Aries

Friends could prove to be helpful in some fairly unexpected ways. Don't turn down their offers of support, even when you have slight doubts about their sincerity. Although you are generally a good judge of character it is possible for you to be wrong sometimes. By the evening you should be in the market for fun.

11 MONDAY
Moon Age Day 27   Moon Sign Taurus

What may be a fairly lucrative financial period is likely to continue now. There is scope for more forward progress and it is easier to get on with those around you than might have been the case recently. A boost to practical matters could so easily come from family members or friends who have especially good ideas.

12 TUESDAY
Moon Age Day 28   Moon Sign Taurus

The demands of the outside world might seem slightly less inviting today. Nobody can keep up the speed of your recent pace indefinitely and Virgo especially does need periods of reflection. Look back on what you have achieved and set today apart in order to enjoy yourself and to luxuriate.

13 WEDNESDAY
Moon Age Day 0   Moon Sign Gemini

You will have little patience when it comes to making compromises at present. In most circumstances this is fine. You know what you want and would be unlikely to make life difficult for others as a result. It is likely that you are feeling filled with energy at present and this shows in most areas of your life.

14 THURSDAY
Moon Age Day 1   Moon Sign Gemini

The potential for financial gain at this time is quite strong. Perhaps you are about to back some scheme or enterprise that has been uppermost in your mind for a while. For whatever reason you are presently very shrewd and anyone who wanted to confuse or fool you now would have to be extremely clever.

15 FRIDAY
Moon Age Day 2   Moon Sign Cancer

Communications are important today. Don't be tardy when it comes to speaking your mind and do whatever you can to buck up the flagging spirits of a friend. All in all this should prove to be both an eventful and interesting period. What might make it better would be a determination to travel.

16 SATURDAY
Moon Age Day 3   Moon Sign Cancer

Inconsequential issues can be distracting but in the main you appear to be getting on rather well in life. Romance offers diversions for some Virgos today, particularly those who are young or young-at-heart. Social diversions will be welcome and a good night out with friends would suit you down to the ground.

17 SUNDAY
Moon Age Day 4   Moon Sign Leo

All sorts of minor pressures and demands could keep you on the go today. There's no letup in the general desire to have fun and no matter what your age you want to participate. Try something new and don't be beaten before you have made the effort. It's very likely that you will surprise yourself before the end of the day.

18 MONDAY
Moon Age Day 5   Moon Sign Leo

Your approach to life is unique this week, but almost certainly successful. People see you as being slightly quirky, but definitely entertaining. Don't spend all of Monday on practical tasks but rather leave some hours during which you can please yourself, whilst offering others a good time too.

19 TUESDAY
Moon Age Day 6   Moon Sign Virgo

The Moon races into your zodiac sign and with everything going for you it is in terms of communication that you can reap the very best sort of benefits right now. There won't be a great deal of time to look over your shoulder today, but it probably isn't necessary in any case. It's onward and upward for Virgo.

20 WEDNESDAY   *Moon Age Day 7   Moon Sign Virgo*

This is the best time of all for starting anything big and for being the star of the show. Although you don't always feel particularly comfortable when circumstances put you on a pedestal, you can certainly show the world what you are made of now. Friendships and romance are two areas on which to concentrate.

21 THURSDAY   *Moon Age Day 8   Moon Sign Libra*

You should be enjoying a fairly successful run if you are a working Virgoan. If not there are gains to be made at home and for all those born under this zodiac sign there is a strong chance of travel. Fresh starts are increasingly likely when it comes to activities outside of work, especially those undertaken alongside friends.

22 FRIDAY   *Moon Age Day 9   Moon Sign Libra*

Keep your eyes open because good news could be coming in from a number of different directions, some of which prove to be quite surprising. You take this in your stride and at the same time you seek change and diversity in your life as a whole. Don't be too surprised if you are singled out for special treatment.

23 SATURDAY   *Moon Age Day 10   Moon Sign Scorpio*

It's a mixed bag today. Although many of your personal ambitions are now clearly on course, don't overstep the mark and expect too much, either of others or yourself. Tread carefully where finances are concerned, and don't push other people into taking financial risks that might frighten them a good deal.

24 SUNDAY   *Moon Age Day 11   Moon Sign Scorpio*

It is fairly clear that you can benefit from someone's advice but this will not be the case unless you listen first. There is a slight tendency for you to plough your own furrow, irrespective of circumstances. Be open in your attitude and don't dismiss alternative strategies simply because they did not occur to you first.

25 MONDAY   *Moon Age Day 12   Moon Sign Scorpio*

Be prepared for a boost coming along as far as your social life is concerned. Together with others, you can make for an interesting time, once the concerns of the material world have been dealt with. You could also notice an upturn in general fortune and financial strength. This should be beginning at any time now.

26 TUESDAY   *Moon Age Day 13   Moon Sign Sagittarius*

It appears that your partner could now play a more dominant role in your life but only because that is the way you want the situation to be. Away from the home, look very carefully at suggestions that are being made which somehow have a bearing on your working circumstances. Perhaps negotiation is necessary.

27 WEDNESDAY   *Moon Age Day 14   Moon Sign Sagittarius*

Keep talking because your powers of communication especially are in the ascendant today and you seem to have what it takes to get your message across to others. If there is a particularly big task before you the best approach today may be to nibble away at the edges of it, or perhaps seek the help of a good friend.

28 THURSDAY   *Moon Age Day 15   Moon Sign Capricorn*

Thursday could be a good time to put financial plans into action, most likely in conjunction with a partner, whether business or personal. As far as romance is concerned, you should be looking out today for someone who is clearly making overtures. Whether you are interested or not remains to be seen, but you should be flattered.

29 FRIDAY   *Moon Age Day 16   Moon Sign Capricorn*

It's quite possible that some hopeful news is on the way, in some instances from far off places. Look at mail carefully. Communication is the key to success as far as Virgo is concerned now and you might even find yourself caught up in email relationships or spending long periods of time on the telephone.

30 SATURDAY   *Moon Age Day 17   Moon Sign Capricorn*

Look out because certain people will be making quite significant demands of you today. If this turns out to be the case you will simply have to refuse some requests, particularly on those occasions when you are sure you are being taken for a mug. Stick up for yourself and you will be respected.

July

2018

1 SUNDAY
Moon Age Day 18   Moon Sign Aquarius

Planetary aspects remain good and there appears to be plenty of challenging cut and thrust to the day. This is particularly true with regard to relationships. Some people who cross your path will be entirely helpful but you can't expect this to be the case universally. Take the ups and downs in your stride – you can learn from them both.

2 MONDAY
Moon Age Day 19   Moon Sign Aquarius

For the first time in ages your love life tends to have its problems right now. For starters you are not so willing or able to see the other person's point of view. Extra flexibility is going to be required and you must do everything you can to examine points that are put to you before you react strongly against them.

3 TUESDAY
Moon Age Day 20   Moon Sign Pisces

As is often the case for you, getting your own way with others is largely a matter of charm, of which you have a great abundance at present. Confidence is growing rapidly, particularly in terms of your forward planning at work. The weather outside should be reasonably good now so get some fresh air.

4 WEDNESDAY
Moon Age Day 21   Moon Sign Pisces

You can't really expect to be number-one today and if you realise why, then disappointments are less likely. This might be a good time for shopping, as long as spending is moderate, and you can also organise things very well, particularly in terms of working practices. Major successes are not all that likely today.

5 THURSDAY
Moon Age Day 22   Moon Sign Pisces

It would be best to opt for some light relief today. There are substantial gains to be made where friendship is concerned, and sociable associations with others could also lead to you discovering ways to get ahead in a financial as well as a personal way. Today starts out slow but should gain speed.

6 FRIDAY
Moon Age Day 23   Moon Sign Aries

Communication matters thrive and intuitive ideas can be brought forward and discussed with a host of different people. If there are any contracts that need signing, now is the time to think about putting pen to paper. You remain extremely astute and will not fail to read the small print – no matter how small it is.

7 SATURDAY
Moon Age Day 24   Moon Sign Aries

At work you now need to follow your instincts – that is if you are even at work on a Saturday. If not, do something different and keep yourself busy and active. With the Sun in its present position just about your best gift is that you can talk and talk. The things you have to say seem important to others and conversations bring new ideas.

8 SUNDAY
Moon Age Day 25   Moon Sign Taurus

Take some time out because domestic relaxation now could ease some of the pressure you might have been feeling at work over the last week. It is more than likely that a family member has some interesting advice for you today. Instead of only half listening, spend an hour or two going through situations with them.

9 MONDAY
Moon Age Day 26   Moon Sign Taurus

In terms of your career this might be a somewhat challenging day. You need to think carefully about long-term motives and to ask yourself if some of the things you are trying to do are strictly necessary. Times could be changing and a new emphasis is possible for Virgo, which might mean letting go of something.

10 TUESDAY   *Moon Age Day 27   Moon Sign Gemini*

Today could be a day filled with more genuine fun than has been the case for a while. Use this interlude to your advantage and without trying to achieve anything in particular, simply have a good time. Those closest to you should be quite happy to join in and you can make the very most of a summer day.

11 WEDNESDAY   *Moon Age Day 28   Moon Sign Gemini*

It is likely that a fairly cautious approach is necessary now where money is concerned, but the same cannot be said in the realm of romance. Here, Virgo is the king or queen. Without thinking, you heap so many compliments on the object of your desire that they will be happy to follow your lead and will be putty in your hands.

12 THURSDAY   *Moon Age Day 29   Moon Sign Cancer*

It's worth paying attention today because the most casual of meetings could turn into something much more interesting. Although there are one or two people around now who are not all that trustworthy, seeing through such individuals isn't at all difficult. The most appealing thing about today is the sheer volume of work you get through.

13 FRIDAY   *Moon Age Day 0   Moon Sign Cancer*

Today offers light relief. Almost anything that is on your personal agenda can prove to be entertaining, particularly in the first part of the day. Later, you return to somewhat quieter ways, and may choose to spend some time on your own, or at least in small groups. Home seems a good place to be this month.

14 SATURDAY   *Moon Age Day 1   Moon Sign Leo*

Look to your instincts because confused situations will follow if you put your faith in the wrong people today. It might be better to follow your own conscience in most matters and to stay away from deliberately provocative types. None of this prevents you from enjoying a generally happy and quite useful sort of Saturday.

15 SUNDAY *Moon Age Day 2   Moon Sign Leo*

You continue to take life in your stride and are unlikely to be fazed by much on what proves to be a fairly sensible sort of Sunday for Virgo. Sensible is fine, but it doesn't create excitement, and you need some of that too. Try not to be willing to settle for second best but push forward progressively.

16 MONDAY *Moon Age Day 3   Moon Sign Virgo*

Many Virgoans will now be feeling more confident and will want to get on with life in as big a way as proves to be possible. The lunar high increases your potential for luck and allows you to go for gold, especially in the workplace. At the same time you are extremely communicative and anxious to talk to almost anyone.

17 TUESDAY *Moon Age Day 4   Moon Sign Virgo*

An active and very energetic time is forecast. You begin Tuesday with the lunar high still in place and will be anxious to prove that you can not only work hard but that you can play hard too. Make the most of the summer weather and perhaps think about taking an outing of some sort – in the company of people you care for.

18 WEDNESDAY *Moon Age Day 5   Moon Sign Libra*

You should be in the best of company today, if only because you are seeking out people you get on with well. The present position of Venus assists you in being as pleasant as can be, a fact that isn't lost on either friends or strangers. Stand by to find your popularity going off the scale.

19 THURSDAY *Moon Age Day 6   Moon Sign Libra*

All aspects of travel can bring pleasure into your life right now. Outdoors, or at home, you know what you want from life and have plenty of energy to get it. What really sets the seal on a good time is the fact that you now find yourself willing to leave behind some of the potential difficulties of the last few days.

20 FRIDAY
Moon Age Day 7   Moon Sign Libra

Though conversations tend to be decidedly pleasant right now you should not allow others to cloud your own judgement, which tends to be very sound at present. Don't rush your fences, especially if there are important decisions to be made. You can afford to take your time in most situations and do so with aplomb.

21 SATURDAY
Moon Age Day 8   Moon Sign Scorpio

Plenty of enjoyable things should be happening in your personal life. This part of July sees at least part of your attention being focused on your love life. If you are between relationships this is the time to keep your eyes open. The behaviour of one person specifically could surprise you.

22 SUNDAY
Moon Age Day 9   Moon Sign Scorpio

Perhaps you don't expect to be the centre of attention all the time today, though there is a definite possibility that this turns out to be the case. Certain actions can lead to disagreements, even though it is plain that you are not being antagonistic. Accept that you can't always be held responsible for the way those around you behave.

23 MONDAY
Moon Age Day 10   Moon Sign Sagittarius

Dealings with a wider social circle this week serve to remind you that your best area of life right now lies in one-to-one pursuits. This is simply because Virgo, though gregarious enough as a rule, needs to deal personally with individuals on occasions. The trend doesn't prevent you from getting on in a practical sense.

24 TUESDAY
Moon Age Day 11   Moon Sign Sagittarius

There is a renewed sense of urgency where specific plans are concerned and you might feel under some sort of pressure, particularly at work. You do tend to take a rather sensible, across the board, attitude to life and this allows you to look rationally at issues that could have been troublesome earlier.

25 WEDNESDAY   *Moon Age Day 12   Moon Sign Capricorn*

Though you are great company for others, you may not have quite the belief in your own abilities that they have in you. It might be sensible to take a look in their direction. If they trust and respect you so much, wouldn't it be sensible to take a leaf from their books? There is very little to lose and much to gain.

26 THURSDAY   *Moon Age Day 13   Moon Sign Capricorn*

You can push ahead in any direction with sufficient confidence to tell you that you know what you are doing. Any small disappointments early in the day are likely to be swamped by much better trends that come along later. The people you care about the most are anxious to spend time with you now.

27 FRIDAY   *Moon Age Day 14   Moon Sign Capricorn*

The accent is on fun and getting together with people who inspire you in some way. Although your attitude is very progressive at present, you will also be going through a slightly nostalgic phase and one that is inclined to prevent you from seeing exactly what lies before you. Take lessons from the past but little else.

28 SATURDAY   *Moon Age Day 15   Moon Sign Aquarius*

Although practical matters are probably running more smoothly than ever, there is some doubt as to personal issues. If this turns out to be the case, you can probably be sure that it is not you who is making waves. Stand by a decision you made earlier, despite the fact that others, particularly younger family members, do not agree.

29 SUNDAY   *Moon Age Day 16   Moon Sign Aquarius*

Trips down memory lane are fine but they don't butter any bread. It is in the world of practicalities that you tend to find yourself today and there are many issues that have to be addressed. Although you remain fairly busy, there should also be more than enough time to find ways in which you can have fun.

30 MONDAY
Moon Age Day 17   Moon Sign Pisces

You feel much easier now about making your way in the world of work. You are fairly fortunate at present because there are plenty of people around who are willing to lend a helping hand when you need it the most. Not every situation can be addressed today however and some patience is necessary.

31 TUESDAY
Moon Age Day 18   Moon Sign Pisces

It will seem to others at this stage of the week that you have a resolution for every problem. Things won't look quite that simple from your point of view but as long as people have faith in your judgement, life will be somewhat easier. Don't turn down a romantic offer without thinking about it carefully.

August

2018

1 WEDNESDAY ☿ *Moon Age Day 19 Moon Sign Pisces*

Some delays are more or less inevitable today and that could mean frustration if you are on the move. All the same, your zodiac sign has the potential to realise that 'everywhere is somewhere' and that you can take pleasure from almost any situation. What you show now are your philosophical qualities.

2 THURSDAY ☿ *Moon Age Day 20 Moon Sign Aries*

Past issues are inclined to arise again now and will cause you to look carefully at your present actions in light of what you did before. It is very important at present to be honest with yourself and not to blinker yourself to what you know is the truth. This could be the start of a solid and a very positive sort of period.

3 FRIDAY ☿ *Moon Age Day 21 Moon Sign Aries*

As if you hadn't noticed, it's high summer now and you ought to be thinking about all those things that need doing around your home whilst the weather is good. Family members will need your special touch today and might be calling a little too freely upon your resources. A gentle reminder could be in order.

4 SATURDAY ☿ *Moon Age Day 22 Moon Sign Taurus*

Whilst decisiveness and quick thinking are usually a bonus, your move towards efficiency in practical matters might be somewhat thwarted today by the actions of those around you. Take a slower and more certain approach because that is the way Virgo usually achieves its most cherished objectives.

5 SUNDAY ☿ *Moon Age Day 23   Moon Sign Taurus*

Right now you definitely benefit from change and variety in your life. Don't settle for second best in anything and be prepared to put in that extra bit of effort that can make all the difference. You will be especially inclined towards travel under present trends and holidays are definitely on the cards for many.

6 MONDAY ☿ *Moon Age Day 24   Moon Sign Gemini*

Get into the habit of planning ahead and then you won't have to rush yourself or decide on your agenda at the last moment. Virgo doesn't like to be pushed into anything and so there are occasions when you will probably dig your heels in, rather than having to do anything that goes against the grain.

7 TUESDAY ☿ *Moon Age Day 25   Moon Sign Gemini*

You don't like getting your hands dirty at the best of times, and especially not right now. Virgo is a cultured zodiac sign and not one that responds well to untidy or cluttered surroundings. For this reason you will probably be spending at least part of today tidying things up – and encouraging other people to do the same.

8 WEDNESDAY ☿ *Moon Age Day 26   Moon Sign Gemini*

Any issues that crop up between yourself and your partner need resolving as quickly as possible. There is a sense of urgency in your life generally and it's clear that you are keen to get on and get things done. Not everyone will be equally helpful at present but the people who count the most remain on your side and offer practical help.

9 THURSDAY ☿ *Moon Age Day 27   Moon Sign Cancer*

Now it looks as though you can gain from productive talks, most likely with people you already know quite well. This would be an ideal phase to start a new regime, so, for example, if you happen to be a smoker, why not think about kicking the habit now? Planetary trends favour change and you are more in the mood to contemplate them.

10 FRIDAY ☿ *Moon Age Day 28   Moon Sign Cancer*

Everyday life will keep you happily on the go and since you are so charming there is little likelihood that you will fall foul of others now. For one thing you are very patient and willing to accept that your own point of view, though perhaps unique, isn't the only one worth considering. Look out for small financial gains later.

11 SATURDAY ☿ *Moon Age Day 0   Moon Sign Leo*

Prepare for what could be a slightly difficult day emotionally. You need to be sure that you understand what others are saying, particularly your partner. As long as you are willing to talk things through steadily, all should be well. What you shouldn't do is fly off the handle without being fully in possession of the facts.

12 SUNDAY ☿ *Moon Age Day 1   Moon Sign Leo*

Your best moments in life today are likely to come as a result of home and family. With less to do in a truly practical sense you can spend a few hours enjoying the time of year and also revelling in the company of those who are closest to you. This should also be a very warm and secure interlude in terms of your romantic life.

13 MONDAY ☿ *Moon Age Day 2   Moon Sign Virgo*

You can certainly afford to be enterprising and enthusiastic today, as the lunar high brings new incentives and plenty of energy into your life. While others are jumping around from foot to foot wondering what you do, you are accomplishing a great deal. Turn towards romance later in the day and make a stupendous impression.

14 TUESDAY ☿ *Moon Age Day 3   Moon Sign Virgo*

Now is definitely the time to rely heavily on your intuition and also to push your luck more than you might have chosen to do for a while. You give a very good impression of yourself, no matter what you decide to do and it is likely that your level of good luck is much higher than it has been so far during August.

15 WEDNESDAY ☿   *Moon Age Day 4   Moon Sign Libra*

Taking the initiative could lead to great successes on the professional front. If you have recently made a decision to clean up your life that's fine but maybe you should lay off the plan somewhat now. With so much going your way it would be best not to starve yourself or reduce other forms of enjoyment excessively.

16 THURSDAY ☿   *Moon Age Day 5   Moon Sign Libra*

Today brings with it a potentially dynamic start. It's true that there are demands around that you cannot fail to address but at the same time you should feel you are making more practical progress than has been possible for a few days. If there are any family parties around – it's time to get your glad rags on.

17 FRIDAY ☿   *Moon Age Day 6   Moon Sign Scorpio*

This is not the sort of day during which you should allow yourself to be diverted from thoughts of personal freedom. Once you have made up your mind to a particular course of action you need to follow it through. Friends and relatives alike should line up to offer whatever help they can at this important time.

18 SATURDAY ☿   *Moon Age Day 7   Moon Sign Scorpio*

Don't allow others to take your present accommodating nature for granted. Although you don't shout about the effort you put in for family and friends, you should point the fact out once or twice today. All it takes is a few words and the positive reaction you get as a result should be more than worth the effort.

19 SUNDAY   *Moon Age Day 8   Moon Sign Sagittarius*

The instinct for skilful money making is strong at the moment. Past efforts have a part to play in this but so do good ideas, which crop up all the time now. Freed from some of the restrictions that you might have felt you were under earlier in the month, it's your own ideas and initiatives that really count now.

20 MONDAY   *Moon Age Day 9   Moon Sign Sagittarius*

The power of your personality is likely to be getting stronger day by day. The promise that comes from your own determination to get on well in life continues to be a central focus and you could also discover that you have new opportunities on offer. Relationships may offer their own potential benefits by the end of the day.

21 TUESDAY   *Moon Age Day 10   Moon Sign Sagittarius*

Avoid tense social situations if you can and keep life light and steady. There are likely to be some surprises in store, though these are hardly going to work against your best interests. Not everyone seems to have your good at heart but when it matters the most you can sort out the sheep from the goats.

22 WEDNESDAY   *Moon Age Day 11   Moon Sign Capricorn*

Don't become waylaid by side issues or gossip. Once you have made up your mind to a particular course of action, keep working hard towards your chosen objectives. It would be sensible to fulfil your promises to others to the best of your ability, though not if that means subverting your own progress.

23 THURSDAY   *Moon Age Day 12   Moon Sign Capricorn*

The art of good conversation is certainly not dead as far as you are concerned. Start today by chatting to just about anyone who will listen and be prepared to be singled out to speak on behalf of others. Your leadership skills are now being recognised, even if you don't consider you have any.

24 FRIDAY   *Moon Age Day 13   Moon Sign Aquarius*

Domestic matters can get in the way of your personal freedom, something you don't want to happen during this Friday. Sort out any minor irritations in the family early on and then you will be free to do whatever takes your fancy. Some Virgos will see this as being a time for turning over a new leaf.

25 SATURDAY
Moon Age Day 14   Moon Sign Aquarius

You may have to focus on minor tasks today because it's the little jobs that add up to successes later on. What matters most about today are the hours when you are not at work. Not only do things look particularly good on the romantic front, but you could also find yourself making a favourable impression on strangers.

26 SUNDAY
Moon Age Day 15   Moon Sign Aquarius

A joint financial venture could prove to be something of a headache so take care that you have thought everything through properly. Meanwhile, there could be events happening in the family that both please and displease you for different reasons. Striking the right balance in your relationships takes tact.

27 MONDAY
Moon Age Day 16   Moon Sign Pisces

Important decisions need to be left alone for the moment. The lunar low is a period you can really enjoy, but only if you are relaxed and willing to go with the flow. Travel could be uppermost in your mind once again and there wouldn't be any harm at all today in seeking out somewhere beautiful to spend a few hours.

28 TUESDAY
Moon Age Day 17   Moon Sign Pisces

For the moment you can get your own way and make life work out more or less the way you would wish. Give yourself a pat on the back for something you have just achieved, but don't allow the situation to go to your head. There is plenty more to do but right now your energy is just a little lacking.

29 WEDNESDAY
Moon Age Day 18   Moon Sign Aries

In a social sense, you appear to be getting along well at the present time. It's true that there will be certain people around you don't care for, but that is always going to be the case. Close friends might prove to be particularly attentive at this time and they offer you insights that will prove to be very important.

30 THURSDAY
Moon Age Day 19   Moon Sign Aries

Try to get away somewhere if you possibly can. Even if you don't have a holiday planned, a shorter change of scene would do you the world of good. What you definitely don't need at this time of year is to be stuck indoors, with no view of nature and no gentle breeze blowing across your face.

31 FRIDAY
Moon Age Day 20   Moon Sign Aries

Your challenge now is to be in the right place to do those things you feel to be important. Don't worry about possible support because that should be around as and when you need it. There are some interesting people crossing your path in the near future and a few of them could turn out to be good friends.

September

1 SATURDAY
Moon Age Day 21   Moon Sign Taurus

This is a time during which your powers of persuasion are extremely good. Mentally speaking you are right on the ball and you have what it takes to turn many situations to your advantage. Not everyone is going to consider you flavour of the month but a fair proportion of people will and it is these individuals that count today.

2 SUNDAY
Moon Age Day 22   Moon Sign Taurus

At home you should find getting along with others to be easy enough. Your partner will be doing all they can to make you happy, efforts you are only too willing to return, leading to an easy-going and conciliatory atmosphere all round. Make at least part of Sunday a time for travelling, even if it is only short distances.

3 MONDAY
Moon Age Day 23   Moon Sign Gemini

Things should still be going well at home, which is probably why you spend as much time there at the moment as you can. With Mars in its present position there could be a few jitters with regard to public appearances, especially if you are expected to speak to a large group of people. Don't worry, you will do fine.

4 TUESDAY
Moon Age Day 24   Moon Sign Gemini

It is at this time that doing your own thing seems most important. There are moments now when you simply don't want to follow the instructions of others, and especially not big heads who you feel don't know what they are talking about. It is necessary to bite your tongue, though the sarcastic side of your nature is could just show.

5 WEDNESDAY   *Moon Age Day 25   Moon Sign Cancer*

A good instinctive understanding of specific situations lies at the heart of your efforts today. Don't allow yourself to be bullied into doing anything that goes against the grain and allow your conscience to rule your decision-making. This should be a good day for romance and for allowing personal matters to run their course.

6 THURSDAY   *Moon Age Day 26   Moon Sign Cancer*

It appears that you will have certain duties to fulfil and not all of them will be equally enjoyable. However, these should not take the edge off your ability to enjoy this day. Although the inclination to travel has been strong within you for some weeks now, today's tendency is more a stay-at-home one.

7 FRIDAY   *Moon Age Day 27   Moon Sign Leo*

This is one of the best times of the month for all social matters and for getting out into the wide world. The good weather isn't over yet and this would be a fine period for a break, even if it's only a short one. Contact with others is important and particularly so when it comes to any sort of personal assignation.

8 SATURDAY   *Moon Age Day 28   Moon Sign Leo*

You could quite easily be feeling restless and perhaps will not welcome the intervention that comes from family and friends. The fact is that you want to be on the move and may not have entirely enjoyed some of the quieter phases of the last week, if these came along for you. Patience is necessary all the same because there are details to be sorted out today.

9 SUNDAY   *Moon Age Day 0   Moon Sign Virgo*

This is the time of the month when good things are likely to happen and when you will be very positive in your outlook. You can afford to push your luck somewhat and you show a very clever face to the world and to most situations. Even if you are working today, don't let it all be about work and make time for fun.

10 MONDAY   *Moon Age Day 1   Moon Sign Virgo*

When it comes to promoting yourself you are second-to-none right now. You will also be extremely capable and can sort out some sort of mess created by others. This won't be difficult and you will probably be surprised at how easily things fall into place. Alongside all this you remain good to know and highly confident.

11 TUESDAY   *Moon Age Day 2   Moon Sign Libra*

There are minor annoyances in career matters today that you probably cannot do a great deal to avoid. Forewarned is forearmed however and you can lessen the impact by taking a few precautions. First and foremost don't try to undertake tasks you know for certain are going to be awkward or annoying.

12 WEDNESDAY   *Moon Age Day 3   Moon Sign Libra*

There are some people around who are not likely to share your bold view of life today. However, you can still gain plenty of admirers simply by being yourself. Don't give in to negative impulses, even if you manage to convince yourself for a while that they are really nothing of the sort.

13 THURSDAY   *Moon Age Day 4   Moon Sign Scorpio*

It could seem today that everyone is demanding your attention at the same time. This situation is far more likely in terms of your social life than in any other aspect of your day-to-day routine. Simply step aside from issues you don't want to deal with at the moment and prepare yourself for a less hurried temporary phase tomorrow.

14 FRIDAY   *Moon Age Day 5   Moon Sign Scorpio*

If it is possible to do so today opt for a total change of scenery. There are social contacts around of the type that you don't often make and also the chance to ring the changes in terms of the places you visit during the day. Stick to what you know is safe today, even if it's not the most exciting option.

15 SATURDAY   *Moon Age Day 6   Moon Sign Scorpio*

Keeping up with the demands of your nearest and dearest, particularly on an emotional level, may not be all that easy. Patience is usually present in the Virgo nature but seems to be taking a holiday for a day or two. All in all, it might be better to spend time on your own rather than upsetting others unintentionally.

16 SUNDAY   *Moon Age Day 7   Moon Sign Sagittarius*

The pace of life should be speeding up now. With so much on your mind and very little time to get everything done, don't fall into the trap of substandard work. This doesn't suit you at all and will be annoying in the longer term. It is far better for you to do one job well than fifteen shabbily.

17 MONDAY   *Moon Age Day 8   Moon Sign Sagittarius*

You may have to focus on minor obligations today and that could take some of the shine off an otherwise positive period. Try to avoid becoming bogged down in issues that are not really relevant to your life and concentrate instead on those matters that put you ahead in the success stakes.

18 TUESDAY   *Moon Age Day 9   Moon Sign Capricorn*

Personal relationships and the way they are presently running prove that you have your work cut out. Keep a sense of proportion when dealing with issues that really are not of that much importance. Most significant of all today is how far you can go when you retain a healthy sense of humour.

19 WEDNESDAY   *Moon Age Day 10   Moon Sign Capricorn*

Practical tasks and run-of-the-mill commitments might not seem to be especially appealing at first today. However, as the hours pass there ought to be some matters that interest you more. What you need eventually is something you can get your teeth into – just a long as it isn't someone!

20 THURSDAY   *Moon Age Day 11   Moon Sign Aquarius*

Although you are clearly filled with exuberance at present there is a slight danger that you may tread on the toes of other people today. Keep yourself busy but spare a few moments to see how your actions are having a bearing on those around you. Putting your thoughts into words isn't likely to be particularly hard at this time.

21 FRIDAY   *Moon Age Day 12   Moon Sign Aquarius*

There are some emotional truths that you will have to come to terms with at present, even if you would rather shy away from them. Don't be too concerned. There are lessons to learn on the way. These will help you make minor modifications to your life, and should lead you to be happier as a result.

22 SATURDAY   *Moon Age Day 13   Moon Sign Aquarius*

Love and romantic developments should be quite important on this September Saturday. Although things might be slightly quieter than during the working week, you have time to look at intimate associations in a new light. If there is one issue that is firmly on your mind today, deal with it as soon as you can – then relax.

23 SUNDAY   *Moon Age Day 14   Moon Sign Pisces*

You might encounter arguments and dissension around you today, though it has to be said that you are not exactly as optimistic yourself as has been the case recently. The lunar low will soon pass and then you can get back to being sweetness and light to everyone. In the meantime it might help to keep a low profile.

24 MONDAY   *Moon Age Day 15   Moon Sign Pisces*

Some partnerships could now seem fraught with emotional baggage, much of which needs to be sorted out and left behind. If a good heart-to-heart can achieve this, then the effort will have been very worthwhile. What you don't need right now is arguments. You won't start them and at this time you may not win them either.

25 TUESDAY
Moon Age Day 16   Moon Sign Aries

Along comes a day when you will largely be doing your own thing and being just what you wish to be. It's important to be comfortable, even if that means making one or two adjustments early in the day. You won't mind catching up with a few routines, just as long as you can do so at your own pace.

26 WEDNESDAY
Moon Age Day 17   Moon Sign Aries

Your emotional responses may not be exactly what you would wish right now. All the more reason not to get involved in arguments or discussions that you cannot hope to win. Be confident in your decision-making, but also be willing to take on board what colleagues and friends have to say.

27 THURSDAY
Moon Age Day 18   Moon Sign Aries

Small issues need to be dealt with early in the day so that you can be really prepared for more important matters later on. If only for this reason don't become frustrated with all the little details of life. The attitudes and opinions of your closest friends have a great part to play in your thinking at the moment.

28 FRIDAY
Moon Age Day 19   Moon Sign Taurus

Matters in the practical world appear to be gearing themselves up for a greater degree of material success. The last couple of weeks have been something of a roller-coaster ride and this general trend shows no sign of diminishing. It's good for you at present to turn your mind outwards, rather than indulging in introspection.

29 SATURDAY
Moon Age Day 20   Moon Sign Taurus

You could be all fingers and thumbs today, which is exactly why you should leave any delicate jobs at least until tomorrow. There are some crucial decisions to be made soon, if not by you, then in your vicinity. If people ask you for your opinion, prepare yourself to tell the truth as you genuinely see it.

30 SUNDAY

Moon Age Day 21   Moon Sign Gemini

Nostalgia might be tugging at your heartstrings on one or two occasions today. Perhaps you are looking at some family photographs or meeting someone you haven't seen for quite some time. Whatever the reason, be aware that life is worth living for now and that there is little future in the past.

October

2018

1 MONDAY
Moon Age Day 22   Moon Sign Gemini

The week starts out well and it looks as though this is going to be a good time for broadening your horizons in some way. Take every opportunity to try something new and don't be held back simply because others don't share your point of view. Avoid family arguments by getting out of the house if necessary and giving yourself space to breathe.

2 TUESDAY
Moon Age Day 23   Moon Sign Cancer

You can afford to indulge your ego today and allow others to make a fuss of you. Your accomplishments look good when viewed through the eyes of family members and friends. Of course you know that you are only part of the way towards some chosen destinations but it's good to know people notice your efforts.

3 WEDNESDAY
Moon Age Day 24   Moon Sign Cancer

Whether you are at work or play today you tend to surround yourself with some interesting people and you should be having a generally good time. Your outgoing and happy nature is definitely on display and that means people generally will be doing all they can for you. This ought to be a rewarding interlude.

4 THURSDAY
Moon Age Day 25   Moon Sign Leo

There seems to be so much happening around you at the moment, especially in your love life, that you can become dizzy with the potential. Away from romance you can make new friendships and also rekindle an old flame that may have burned lower recently. Don't be surprised if you are flavour of the month to many people.

135

5 FRIDAY
Moon Age Day 26   Moon Sign Leo

Now you are more than willing to put in the time and effort to anything you see as being necessary to your own well being and that of those you care for. Once again you should find that romance is high on your agenda and also that of your partner. If you have just started a new relationship things should be going well.

6 SATURDAY
Moon Age Day 27   Moon Sign Virgo

With the lunar high comes a certainty in your mind that you are going in the right direction generally speaking. Take advantage of every opportunity to make a good impression and be prepared to push your luck as much as you can. There is room for variation in your schedule today, which the position of the Moon supports.

7 SUNDAY
Moon Age Day 28   Moon Sign Virgo

Now filled with optimism and high spirits, you need to make today special in some way. Giving others a helping hand might not be a bad start and you should also be thinking in terms of changes you can make in and around your home. Best of all you feel the need to get out and party – if you can find someone willing to join in.

8 MONDAY
Moon Age Day 29   Moon Sign Virgo

Your concern now turns towards orderliness in the workplace. It's clear that at the moment you want things to be just so and you won't have a great deal of patience with anyone who seems to be throwing a spanner in the works. In a social sense your tidy mind is put to good use in sorting out the mess created by a friend.

9 TUESDAY
Moon Age Day 0   Moon Sign Libra

You tend to meet obstacles of any sort with patience and a good sense of humour, which is probably more than can be said for certain other people in your vicinity. Most of the time you could feel that you have to rely on yourself and that those around you are not working efficiently or sensibly. Continue to offer support.

10 WEDNESDAY *Moon Age Day 1   Moon Sign Libra*

Look out for the chance to make new friends, as well as ways of strengthening personal ties. Not everyone is going to be on your side in practical matters but you have winning ways and a very persuasive nature at this time. On the rare occasion when you can't bring others round to your point of view, carry on with what you believe in anyway.

11 THURSDAY *Moon Age Day 2   Moon Sign Scorpio*

If there are changes coming along in your working environment you should take these on board and even welcome them if you can. Virgo, like all Earth signs, tends to stick to what it knows but this can be a negative reaction sometimes. You need to be progressive and to embrace new technologies and improved techniques.

12 FRIDAY *Moon Age Day 3   Moon Sign Scorpio*

You should have a positive and compromising attitude today, which makes others instinctively trust and like you. Popularity is not too hard for the average Virgo to find, even if you sometimes think you are not all that well loved by friends. What you always need is more self-confidence, which is present in your chart today.

13 SATURDAY *Moon Age Day 4   Moon Sign Sagittarius*

Extended talks and general negotiations seem to be the order of the day. Some of these will prove to be very useful, while others don't offer quite the rewards you may have been expecting. Treat each situation on its own merits and don't be too alarmed if some people appear to be quite disruptive. Things can be sorted out.

14 SUNDAY *Moon Age Day 5   Moon Sign Sagittarius*

Ideas, plans and thoughts should flow smoothly between yourself and others. This would therefore be an excellent time for working in partnerships or for getting involved in new ventures that involve colleagues. Friends also have some good ideas and you will probably want to be involved in these from the start.

15 MONDAY   *Moon Age Day 6   Moon Sign Capricorn*

At this time you are a very creative person and you can best satisfy your own personal goals by trying new things. You will want to be surrounded by order and, if possible, luxury, something that is always close to the Virgo heart. You may also be keen to make some changes at home, alongside family members.

16 TUESDAY   *Moon Age Day 7   Moon Sign Capricorn*

There could be some slight difficulties at work today. Maybe you are not communicating as well with others as would normally be the case. Have some patience in your dealings with other people, a few of whom could appear to be playing rather silly games. Socially, life should be secure enough.

17 WEDNESDAY   *Moon Age Day 8   Moon Sign Capricorn*

There is good potential for attracting new people into your life, either at work or socially. The middle of the working week is quite likely to bring you into contact with types who can be of specific use to you practically, though by the evening you will be opting to let your hair down and have some fun.

18 THURSDAY   *Moon Age Day 9   Moon Sign Aquarius*

You should have little or no trouble staying in the good books of others today. You are popular with others and it appears that you know exactly what to say in order to get the right sort of reactions. Campaigns that you have embarked upon need dealing with very carefully. Don't rush into anything.

19 FRIDAY   *Moon Age Day 10   Moon Sign Aquarius*

Socially speaking you are now likely to be drawn to the new and unusual in life. Not that there is all that much time to take notice of it today. Life is hectic, probably because of the needs that others have of you. There are moments when rules and regulations could get on your nerves if you can't find ways to ignore them.

20 SATURDAY   *Moon Age Day 11   Moon Sign Pisces*

This is a time during which you are challenged to overcome negative thinking and that's fine but make sure you bear in mind that so many of your plans might not look all that workable over the next couple of days. Don't take any prohibitive action until later and, in the meantime, try to let things ride if you can.

21 SUNDAY   *Moon Age Day 12   Moon Sign Pisces*

It could seem that no matter how hard you try you are getting nowhere fast. This is because you continue to knock your head against a very unnecessary wall. Stand and watch on the riverbank of life, rather than jumping into the water. The more you relax, the better you will deal with these slightly negative astrological circumstances.

22 MONDAY   *Moon Age Day 13   Moon Sign Pisces*

Though group and co-operative ventures tend to go smoothly enough today it is in the direction of personal relationships that your mind turns. Mixing freely with your friends, you could discover that one or two of them hold a key that can open some very interesting doors for you.

23 TUESDAY   *Moon Age Day 14   Moon Sign Aries*

There are some wonderful surprises in store for Virgo today, but you will have to keep your eye on the ball to gain from any of them. Trends indicate that not everyone is on your side in the workplace, but those who are not probably have something to gain from opposing you. Don't rise to the bait!

24 WEDNESDAY   *Moon Age Day 15   Moon Sign Aries*

You definitely enjoy being busy today and can make the best out of almost any sort of circumstance. Watch out for the odd minor mishap, probably brought about as a result of carelessness exhibited by someone else. Your present quick thinking makes you good to have around in any tight corner.

25 THURSDAY *Moon Age Day 16   Moon Sign Taurus*

Now is the time to be enjoying good social trends and to be letting people know just how capable you are. It may not be particularly easy to control all aspects of your life, but you care less about certain issues at this time. Your insight into relationships should help them to work out particularly well.

26 FRIDAY *Moon Age Day 17   Moon Sign Taurus*

Right now, making up your mind regarding even a crucial personal matter is not going to be at all easy. It might be best to defer decisions until later. By that time you will have had the chance to seek out the advice of someone you trust implicitly. Friends are easy to make at this time, and are not likely to be lost later.

27 SATURDAY *Moon Age Day 18   Moon Sign Gemini*

Talks with others can find you making the sort of headway you hadn't been expecting. For many Virgos this is a day of rest, but this may not appeal to you on this particular Saturday. As a result, don't be surprised to find yourself out of bed early and anxious to get on with life just as quickly as you are able.

28 SUNDAY *Moon Age Day 19   Moon Sign Gemini*

You may discover that some people are far less assertive than usual, and you can put that down to your own attitude. It is a fact that you don't brook any interference right now and that those around you get the message. The more you get done very early today, the greater is the likelihood that you can enjoy a peaceful Sunday.

29 MONDAY *Moon Age Day 20   Moon Sign Cancer*

Emotions could be quite close to the surface now, which is a state of affairs Virgo does not like too much. Although you are generally warm, the innermost workings of your nature tend to be hidden. Feeling like a sheet of glass is not especially comfortable for anyone born under your zodiac sign.

30 TUESDAY   *Moon Age Day 21   Moon Sign Cancer*

A friend or social contact is likely to be trying your patience now. It would be good to spread your influence socially and there is certainly no need to fall out with anyone. Social trends remain generally good but it's likely that you will be turning more and more to family members in order to fill your quiet hours at present.

31 WEDNESDAY   *Moon Age Day 22   Moon Sign Cancer*

There are some curious situations around at the moment and since you wish to resolve them, a little detective work may be in order. Make certain that you are not wasting time on needless distractions because there is enough to do now without going down pointless roads. Scrutinise carefully any documents that need signing.

November
2018

1 THURSDAY
Moon Age Day 23   Moon Sign Leo

You could now be sensing some fairly inevitable changes in your life and it would be good to know that it was you deciding what should alter. Think deeply about certain aspects and take advice from people in the know. Trends indicate that November may be a very eventful month for you.

2 FRIDAY
Moon Age Day 24   Moon Sign Leo

Your creativity may be enhanced now and whether you are working or not this Friday you want to make things look and feel beautiful. Enlisting the support of family members, and especially your partner, should be fairly easy and together you can enjoy whatever you are doing. A trip away from your home environment seems likely.

3 SATURDAY
Moon Age Day 25   Moon Sign Virgo

Look around carefully because a word in the right ear can work virtual miracles at present. Give yourself fully to all that the day has to offer, particularly if you awaken with a feeling of concern that things may not be going your way. Making progress in matters of the heart and really enjoying yourself are what today is about.

4 SUNDAY
Moon Age Day 26   Moon Sign Virgo

You will be able to take full advantage of almost any situation now. With friends willing to do what they can to assist, you embark on a distinctly social day, with plenty of enjoyment possible and some financial gains also in evidence. Don't be tardy when it comes to expressing an opinion.

5 MONDAY
Moon Age Day 27   Moon Sign Libra

The accent today is more or less totally on fun and pleasure, even if you have to go to work. You can make any situation enjoyable and will want to involve others in many of your zany schemes. Virgo is light-hearted and fun-loving in almost everything now and it will be quite difficult for you to take any aspect of life completely seriously.

6 TUESDAY
Moon Age Day 28   Moon Sign Libra

Your main focus now remains on doing what you can to help others, though your attitude isn't entirely charitable because you are doing yourself some good on the way. Have some fun during today and get together with like-minded people whenever you can. You should also find time to show how romantic you are.

7 WEDNESDAY
Moon Age Day 0   Moon Sign Scorpio

Your generally contented outlook on life makes you popular with just about everyone today and allows you to push the bounds of the possible when it comes to getting those around you to do what you want. A little cheek can go a long way and you could end up very surprised at just how much you can influence people.

8 THURSDAY
Moon Age Day 1   Moon Sign Scorpio

Now you are a natural detective as you seek to ferret out the truth. Today can be interesting and useful when it comes to discovering what is really going on around you and there could be some surprises regarding the behaviour of a family member or a friend. In the main you should be fairly happy and contented with your own lot.

9 FRIDAY
Moon Age Day 2   Moon Sign Sagittarius

Virgo is on form and it is now easy for you to shine in personal matters, during a period that is excellent regarding your closest attachments. Where there has been a little discord, now you find reconciliation and warmth. It may not be your own attitude that has changed at all but rather the ideas and opinions of others.

10 SATURDAY *Moon Age Day 3   Moon Sign Sagittarius*

Things just seem to get better. Friendship and group encounters generally appear to have a great deal going for them right now. What they provide is a platform for your ego, perhaps at a time when you are not quite as confident in yourself as has been the case of late. Make time to socialise, particularly by the evening.

11 SUNDAY *Moon Age Day 4   Moon Sign Sagittarius*

It looks as though consolidation is the key to getting on well right now. Instead of firing off with new ideas, look carefully at the ones you have been addressing recently. It might take only a very small amount of effort to put the seal on weeks or months of work. On the way through life today new friends are a possibility.

12 MONDAY *Moon Age Day 5   Moon Sign Capricorn*

Everyday issues should keep you happily on the go today and although this time may not be exactly startling as far as you are concerned, it should be reasonably enjoyable. Try not to allow yourself to be bogged down by details that don't really matter and avoid worrying about people who are doing fine. Keep up new efforts.

13 TUESDAY *Moon Age Day 6   Moon Sign Capricorn*

You can be a definite agent for change today if you apply yourself properly. You are a natural reformer and can do things now that will improve the lot of others, as well as having a significant bearing on your own life. Where money is concerned you could have been fairly conservative recently but should be more of a gambler now.

14 WEDNESDAY *Moon Age Day 7   Moon Sign Aquarius*

This would be a very fortunate time for business discussions and for making alterations to the way you do things in a practical sense. It could be that you now recognise you have been chasing some sort of rainbow recently. This leads to more concerted action and a definite change of emphasis now and for the days to come.

15 THURSDAY   *Moon Age Day 8   Moon Sign Aquarius*

Now you are constantly looking for new opportunities and showing the world at large just how much savvy you have. It should still be easy to get others to back you in your schemes and you have a great deal of resolve when dealing with those in authority. The occasional shyness of Virgo is definitely not on display right now.

16 FRIDAY   *Moon Age Day 9   Moon Sign Aquarius*

Your social life might be something of a letdown at the moment. If so, you probably are not dealing with certain people in the right way. Certainly you should not allow yourself to be held back by negative attitudes. Leave alone those individuals who insist on taking a pessimistic approach to life.

17 SATURDAY   ☿   *Moon Age Day 10   Moon Sign Pisces*

It would not be in the least surprising to find that you lack energy today or that you cannot get yourself motivated in the way you wish. Let others do some of the hard work, while you sit back and supervise. You are still making your own choices and as far as your determination is concerned very little seems to have changed.

18 SUNDAY   ☿   *Moon Age Day 11   Moon Sign Pisces*

It is likely that you will feel pulled in different directions today. Your loyalty lies in more than one place and so deciding who you should please may not be easy. While the Moon is in Pisces it is probably best not to try. You are not quite as ingenious right now as you have been, or as you will be in the days ahead.

19 MONDAY   ☿   *Moon Age Day 12   Moon Sign Aries*

Along comes a day for positive social relations and one that finds you distinctly more up front than appears to have been the case yesterday. Sort out any routines early in the day and don't be afraid to have some fun. Others may notice how much you tease at present, but this is hardly likely to be a stumbling block.

20 TUESDAY ☿ *Moon Age Day 13   Moon Sign Aries*

When things get quiet, Virgos might spend time pampering themselves. Why not? You have put in a great deal of effort in the recent past and you deserve to have a decent rest. If, on the other hand, you have to work today, do as little as you can and allow others to fill in where possible. This could be a fairly uneventful day.

21 WEDNESDAY ☿ *Moon Age Day 14   Moon Sign Taurus*

You will most likely actively choose to be on the move during the course of your daily affairs for the moment. Staying in one place and doing exactly what is expected of you is hardly likely to be much fun and there is so much scope for having a good time it seems rather pointless to restrict yourself unduly.

22 THURSDAY ☿ *Moon Age Day 15   Moon Sign Taurus*

Career matters that lack direction should be dealt with firmly and immediately right now. Don't let things stew in your life generally and be willing to take the sort of decisions that you know to be sensible. Your attitude towards loved ones varies, especially if some of them are being deliberately awkward.

23 FRIDAY ☿ *Moon Age Day 16   Moon Sign Taurus*

Your social life could prove to be rather testy and this means that you have to question certain relationships and what they are presently offering you. Try to examine the overall effect you are having on others but don't judge yourself too harshly. In all situations those around you can be wrong too.

24 SATURDAY ☿ *Moon Age Day 17   Moon Sign Gemini*

Your persuasive powers over others are pretty strong today, so if there is anything you really want, now is the time to go out and ask for it. It won't be as simple as that of course, though nobody you care for will refuse reasonable requests. Socially speaking you seem to be reaching a high and may be planning ahead well.

25 SUNDAY ☿ *Moon Age Day 18* *Moon Sign Gemini*

The pursuit of wealth might now be on your list of priorities. Virgo may not be the most acquisitive of the zodiac signs, but it isn't too far behind. It's all down to a sense of security, which Virgo desires. Casting your mind forward in time, you can now do some deals that will suit your needs in years to come.

26 MONDAY ☿ *Moon Age Day 19* *Moon Sign Cancer*

Stay clear of disagreements today if you can possibly manage to do so. It would be better not to interact too much with people at all, rather than to find yourself involved in pointless rows. Such a state of affairs is far less likely in terms of deep attachments. Virgos who are looking for love should have some success now.

27 TUESDAY ☿ *Moon Age Day 20* *Moon Sign Cancer*

Compromise is your middle name today, or at least it if isn't, then it should be. You can get more today by being willing to give a little than at just about any other time this month. Some nostalgia creeps in, but that is part of the way present trends make themselves felt in your life. Soon you will be flying high again.

28 WEDNESDAY ☿ *Moon Age Day 21* *Moon Sign Leo*

On a practical level, you are quite pressured, but this fact will not prevent you from getting on well all the same. Out here in the middle of the week, and in the midst of some demanding situations, there are people who buckle under the pressure. You, fortunately, are not one of them. Give what support you can.

29 THURSDAY ☿ *Moon Age Day 22* *Moon Sign Leo*

Social encounters look good and are inclined to inspire you to try new possibilities. There are opportunities to meet people who may be in a good position to offer you advice and the association you have with others at this time could start your mind thinking along lines that haven't been available in the past.

30 FRIDAY   ☿   *Moon Age Day 23   Moon Sign Virgo*

Changing solar influences come along now that stimulate your natural curiosity regarding the world and the way it runs. It would be sensible to allow professionals, or people you feel to be superior, know of your own thoughts today. Even the most casual remarks you make are likely to be taken on board.

♍ December 2018

1 SATURDAY ☿ *Moon Age Day 24   Moon Sign Virgo*

This Saturday puts a spring in your step and a smile firmly on your face. The fact is that with the lunar high about you are the life and soul of any party. Friends and relatives alike seem to be doing all they can to make you happy now, though most of the effort is clearly coming from your direction.

2 SUNDAY ☿ *Moon Age Day 25   Moon Sign Libra*

You may now be in discussion regarding an emotional matter and it's a fact that much of what is happening today will be associated with your home. Things can be solved quite easily just as long as you are willing to talk and with Mercury in its present position that should hardly be a problem.

3 MONDAY ☿ *Moon Age Day 26   Moon Sign Libra*

Someone might be trying to put you down in the minds of others, or at least that's how it will appear to you right now. It is likely that you are not looking at things quite as logically as would normally be the case and emotions can get in the way. Most importantly, keep a smile on your face, even when you feel jumpy.

4 TUESDAY ☿ *Moon Age Day 27   Moon Sign Scorpio*

It seems as though you will be looking for a more advantageous social position as you entertain others and keep people smiling throughout most of today. You generally have an interesting story to tell and it won't be hard for you to maintain your standing as the centre of attention. Your personal life should take a turn for the better now.

5 WEDNESDAY ☿ *Moon Age Day 28* *Moon Sign Scorpio*

Self-determination on your part paves the way towards achieving personal goals around this time. Put your best foot forward in all practical matters especially and show the world just how capable you can be. Later in the day you should find that the romantic responses coming your way are not quite what you expected.

6 THURSDAY ☿ *Moon Age Day 29* *Moon Sign Scorpio*

Today's personal news may put you nicely in touch with the wider world and this in turn reminds you of concerns that exist a long way from your own front door. You become a more charitable animal at this time of year and will want to do what you can to help those who are less well off than you are. Virgo is definitely a caring sign at present.

7 FRIDAY *Moon Age Day 0* *Moon Sign Sagittarius*

Today could be a good time to focus on the very practical aspects of life. Roll up your sleeves and get cracking this Friday, sorting out all those issues that have been left on the shelf for a while. It's part of clearing the decks ahead of the holidays and it is something that Virgo is inclined to do regularly at this time of year.

8 SATURDAY *Moon Age Day 1* *Moon Sign Sagittarius*

You tend to be quite outspoken now so if you are involved in discussions it is possible that you will have to guard your tongue. Speaking out of turn now could bring problems further down the road. The right sort of circumstances to allow material progress may not be present at first but they soon develop later.

9 SUNDAY *Moon Age Day 2* *Moon Sign Capricorn*

It looks as though challenges will come along at this time, though most of them are welcome since they offer you the chance to show exactly what you are made of. The objections that others might make about your life may only serve to show where their own faults lie. For this reason alone it isn't worth rising to the bait.

10 MONDAY *Moon Age Day 3 Moon Sign Capricorn*

Since you need to express yourself fully now there's a chance you will be so busy talking that you will overlook a few fairly important details. This isn't like you as a rule but then nobody is perfect! What might really get your goat at the moment are rules and regulations for which you can see no real justification.

11 TUESDAY *Moon Age Day 4 Moon Sign Aquarius*

Matters of the heart should be a genuine source of support and happiness today. Although this means that you may not be keeping your eye on the ball as much as usual in a practical sense, all should be well in your world as a whole. Some forward planning regarding the holiday season can now be addressed.

12 WEDNESDAY *Moon Age Day 5 Moon Sign Aquarius*

Socially speaking you could now find yourself entering a short lull. Others are grumpy or difficult to deal with and a great deal of patience is necessary. On the other hand you could choose instead to spend a few hours on your own. Those born under the sign of Virgo are quite happy to go it alone now and then.

13 THURSDAY *Moon Age Day 6 Moon Sign Aquarius*

Things change and socially speaking you ought to be fairly impressive now. There are plenty of people around on whom you can try out your present skills and since most of them appear to care for you the job should be easy. However, you might find that it is more of a problem to deal with arising difficulties at work.

14 FRIDAY *Moon Age Day 7 Moon Sign Pisces*

If there are challenges in emotional relationships just now you can thank the lunar low for them. Nothing that happens at present is likely to shake your equilibrium too much and your presently forgiving nature is still very much present. It might be best not to push yourself too hard and to be willing to take a little rest right now.

15 SATURDAY   *Moon Age Day 8   Moon Sign Pisces*

It could feel as if you are not totally in charge of your own destiny at this stage of the week and that can make you rather uncertain and somewhat hesitant. Don't worry because these trends are very temporary. By tomorrow you should be right back on form but for the moment you may have to rely more heavily on other people.

16 SUNDAY   *Moon Age Day 9   Moon Sign Pisces*

Today you tend to feel very sociable and easy-going as the worst excesses of the lunar low disappear completely. With Christmas firmly in your sights you will be socialising a lot more than might have been the case earlier in the month and it also looks as though you will be quite busy in every practical sense at the moment.

17 MONDAY   *Moon Age Day 10   Moon Sign Aries*

What an ideal time this is to be out there in the social mainstream of life. Parties and gatherings of any sort appeal to you because you are presently the life and soul of any function. However, be careful how much you eat and drink because otherwise you may end up regretting your tendency towards excess.

18 TUESDAY   *Moon Age Day 11   Moon Sign Aries*

Along comes a time for capitalising on all recent advances at work. It really is time to strike while the iron is hot and to do things before Christmas actually arrives. In a family sense not everyone is likely to be equally helpful and many of the everyday responsibilities appear to be falling on you.

19 WEDNESDAY   *Moon Age Day 12   Moon Sign Taurus*

Your approach to certain emotional matters might not be as positive as you had first intended. If this turns out to be the case you will simply have to try again. Realising that you are capable of getting it wrong is the first step on an important inward journey. Social trends still look good and enjoyment is on the cards.

20 THURSDAY   *Moon Age Day 13   Moon Sign Taurus*

Any number of speculative matters could turn your way right now and you can afford to take the odd little chance in life. As the day wears on it is likely that you will be running out of steam physically, though it's clear that your mind is working well and that you are in a position to offer some sound advice.

21 FRIDAY   *Moon Age Day 14   Moon Sign Gemini*

Compromises in relationships are a natural part of what you will encounter at the present time. If you refuse to make them, problems could come along later. Stay away from rows in your family, or indeed amongst friends. The problem is not one of failing to hold your own, but rather being too aggressive.

22 SATURDAY   *Moon Age Day 15   Moon Sign Gemini*

Get ready to make tracks and get ahead professionally. With one eye on Christmas and the other on what you want to achieve materially, there isn't a great deal of time to spare right now. Don't overbook yourself for the forthcoming days. There may be shopping to do today that you had forgotten.

23 SUNDAY   *Moon Age Day 16   Moon Sign Cancer*

Getting along with others isn't too difficult this Sunday, just as long as they are willing to do more or less exactly what you ask. The fact is that you are being rather more selfish than would normally be the case. Get out and about if you can, though it is likely that your main destination will still be the local shopping centre.

24 MONDAY   *Moon Age Day 17   Moon Sign Cancer*

The emotional rewards from intimate relationships are showing much more clearly now. Your confidence rises as you realise that people are really listening to what you have to say. Go for what you want and be willing to grab the odd chance that under normal circumstances you may shy away from.

25 TUESDAY
Moon Age Day 18   Moon Sign Leo

You should definitely be feeling at your best today. The people who matter the most are around you and Christmas Day has much to offer in terms of genuine warmth and affection. Don't forget obligations to those who can't be with you at this time and remain at your charitable best generally.

26 WEDNESDAY
Moon Age Day 19   Moon Sign Leo

Social developments are now positively highlighted, allowing you to make the most of the time between now and the New Year. Virgo becomes quite the party animal and you know how to help others to have a good time too. The everyday responsibilities of life are now shelved.

27 THURSDAY
Moon Age Day 20   Moon Sign Virgo

It cannot get much better than having the lunar high present during the Christmas holidays. You should be filled with beans and anxious to get as much out of life as you possibly can. People will warm to your infectious humour and to the fact that you put yourself out so much on their behalf. This should be a really good day.

28 FRIDAY
Moon Age Day 21   Moon Sign Virgo

This is the best part of the month for fresh starts and for getting ahead with unfinished work. Everything goes with a swing now and you can impress people as easily as falling off a log. Your popularity ought to be high and because you are not in the mood for work you will certainly show others that you know how to have a good time.

29 SATURDAY
Moon Age Day 22   Moon Sign Libra

Stick to the simple things of life and spend some time spoiling yourself. There is an active and very demanding period ahead, so it won't do you any harm to charge up those batteries. Your confidence should not be dented unless you come face to face with people who seem determined to put you down.

30 SUNDAY
Moon Age Day 23   Moon Sign Libra

Things remain generally positive. You score many points in social situations, especially so if you are away from home and enjoying the hospitality of others. Try not to be critical about the way those around you arrange their functions and simply pitch in. Too much fussing won't get you anywhere today so try to stay very relaxed.

31 MONDAY
Moon Age Day 24   Moon Sign Libra

New Year's Eve brings you to thinking quite deeply about what you have achieved and you will also be carefully planning what comes next. That's fine during the day but by the time the evening arrives you will have other things to do. Enjoy whatever party you go to and stay in the company of people who you care for deeply.

RISING SIGNS FOR VIRGO

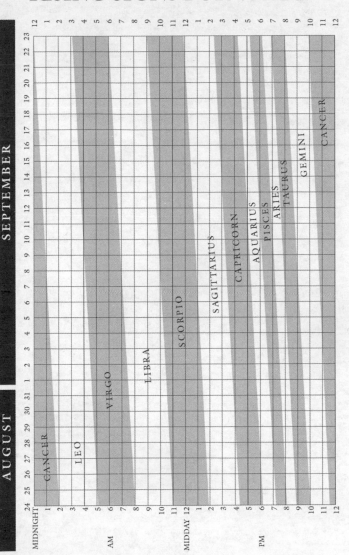

THE ZODIAC, PLANETS AND CORRESPONDENCES

The Earth revolves around the Sun once every calendar year, so when viewed from Earth the Sun appears in a different part of the sky as the year progresses. In astrology, these parts of the sky are divided into the signs of the zodiac and this means that the signs are organised in a circle. The circle begins with Aries and ends with Pisces.

Taking the zodiac sign as a starting point, astrologers then work with all the positions of planets, stars and many other factors to calculate horoscopes and birth charts and tell us what the stars have in store for us.

The table below shows the planets and Elements for each of the signs of the zodiac. Each sign belongs to one of the four Elements: Fire, Air, Earth or Water. Fire signs are creative and enthusiastic; Air signs are mentally active and thoughtful; Earth signs are constructive and practical; Water signs are emotional and have strong feelings.

It also shows the metals and gemstones associated with, or corresponding with, each sign. The correspondence is made when a metal or stone possesses properties that are held in common with a particular sign of the zodiac.

Finally, the table shows the opposite of each star sign – this is the opposite sign in the astrological circle.

Placed	Sign	Symbol	Element	Planet	Metal	Stone	Opposite
1	Aries	Ram	Fire	Mars	Iron	Bloodstone	Libra
2	Taurus	Bull	Earth	Venus	Copper	Sapphire	Scorpio
3	Gemini	Twins	Air	Mercury	Mercury	Tiger's Eye	Sagittarius
4	Cancer	Crab	Water	Moon	Silver	Pearl	Capricorn
5	Leo	Lion	Fire	Sun	Gold	Ruby	Aquarius
6	Virgo	Maiden	Earth	Mercury	Mercury	Sardonyx	Pisces
7	Libra	Scales	Air	Venus	Copper	Sapphire	Aries
8	Scorpio	Scorpion	Water	Pluto	Plutonium	Jasper	Taurus
9	Sagittarius	Archer	Fire	Jupiter	Tin	Topaz	Gemini
10	Capricorn	Goat	Earth	Saturn	Lead	Black Onyx	Cancer
11	Aquarius	Waterbearer	Air	Uranus	Uranium	Amethyst	Leo
12	Pisces	Fishes	Water	Neptune	Tin	Moonstone	Virgo